Marvella Nomine is an author, mother and admirer of all badasses. She lives in London.

MARVELLA NOMINE

Badass Baby Names

INSPIRED BY
THE MOST AWESOME FEARLESS COOL
MEN & WOMEN IN HISTORY

HEAD
of ZEUS

An Anima Book

This is an Anima book, first published in the UK in 2019
by Head of Zeus Ltd

9 7 5 3 1 2 4 6 8

A catalogue record for this book is available from
the British Library.

ISBN (TPBO): 9781788542869
ISBN (E): 9781788542852

Printed and bound in Great Britain by
CPI Group (UK) Ltd, Croydon CR0 4YY

Head of Zeus Ltd
First Floor East
5–8 Hardwick Street
London EC1R 4RG

WWW.HEADOFZEUS.COM

CONTENTS

Before you dive in...

Disclaimer! I have tried to be as historically accurate as possible, but this is a badass baby name book and not a scholarly piece of excellence, so please excuse the odd embellishment or factual error. Soz in advance if you find any.**

Disclaimer #2: I apologize for the unnecessary swearing, overuse of the phrases *boundary busting, kicked ass, smashed the patriarchy* and abundance of clichés. This is a lighthearted badass baby name book so if you don't like it, just chill the fuck out.**

Disclaimer #3: if you decide to go ahead and call your baby after the total boss that is Jezza Corbyn, that's amazing! But don't blame me when you later realize you have a baby named Jeremy and it is no longer 1954.**

And finally...

Bringing a small human into the world is one of the most awesome and epically terrifying adventures. Let's be honest, parents are already badasses in the Xtreme. And through all the shitty sleepless nights, endless crying (mostly yours) and worries, the magic of this little life-changing juggernaut will fill your heart with so much joy that whatever name you eventually choose, I promise you it will be absolutely perfect. Because it belongs to your baby!*

* Jeremy included.

Badass Badges

Activist

Bat-shit crazy

Boundary-busting badass

Brave

Designer

Fearless adventurer

Freakin' awesome

Gave death the finger

Gave no fucks

Hard as nails

Hear me roar

Hero

Leader

Lifesaver

Mad skillz

Performer

Pirate

Powerhouse

Record-breaker

Royalty – queen/king/princess/prince

Sassy AF (that's sassy as fuck)

Saved the world

Scientist

Smart AF (smart as fuck)

Smashed the patriarchy

Spy

Thrill-seeker

Trailblazer

Warrior

World-changer

Badass Xtreme: ***** rating

ABRAHAM (ABE)

Want your future son to grow up honest, with morals in abundance, unafraid to climb the highest of mountains in order to achieve justice? Why not name him after the benevolent, Union-saving, war-hating, slavery-slaying, equal rights activist and American hero, Abraham Lincoln (1809–65)?

From humble beginnings on a poor farm in southern Indiana, he became one of the most boundary-busting presidents in US history. Abraham was a self-taught lawyer and became notorious as a tough-talking, ball-busting cross-examiner, delivering Oscar-worthy closing arguments. He lost five elections before becoming president of the United States in 1860. During his time in office, he fought hard for women's rights and social justice; he abolished slavery, saved the Union during the Civil War and created the secret service on the day of his assassination.

A man who could also storm a wrestling ring like a WWE pro, Abe is enshrined in the Wrestling Hall of Fame, having lost just 1 match in 300: total respect.

BADASS RATING: ★★★★★
A world-changing crusader who could also grow an impressive beard.

ADA

Will your little squidge be a mathematics maven? A princess of parallelograms, queen of Quine and countess of computers? Then name her after Ada Lovelace (1815–52).

It was while Ada was casually translating an Italian paper on the theory behind Charles Babbage's computers or 'analytical engines' (as they were then known) that her legacy was built. She ignored the musings of her male peers who were too focused on merely crunching numbers, and declared that machines can do anything, given the right programming and input. Ada could not help but add her own notes to the paper she was translating, arguing that music and pictures could be interpreted into a digital language that could be read by a machine – and basically published the world's first ever algorithm to demonstrate so!

Ada's annotated paper went on to influence Alan Turing almost a century later and formed the foundation for modern computer science.

BADASS RATING: ★★★★★
Intelligent and independent, Ada's ideas were fiercely ahead of their time.

ADELINE

Want to name your little one after a leather-clad badass who, along with her sister, blazed across America on a motorbike to make a stand against patriarchy and prove that women can do absolutely anything men can do? Yes? Well, give her the namesake Adeline Van Buren (1894–1953).

Adeline and her sister Augusta Van Buren both wanted to become military dispatch riders, but at the time women were not allowed to serve in combat for the US army. So the sisters stuck two fingers up to the notion that only a man could handle a job as dangerous as feeding information to the front line and plotted a journey across the then-treacherous continent of America to prove just how badass women can be.

In 1916 Gussie and Addie donned leather riding breeches and leggings and rode over 5,500 miles from New York City to Ohio, across Indiana, Illinois and Iowa and beyond; they revved engines over the Rocky Mountains, powered through heavy rain and swamping mud and navigated dirt trails and steep inclines with total boss-like skillz. From the fish springs of Utah to the deserts of Nevada, across the bridges of San Francisco, down to the border city of Tijuana, the sisters smashed records, fought off arrests and persevered through epic conditions. In just sixty days they reached Mexico, kicking the ass of America and proving that, 'She can, if she will.'

BADASS RATING: ★★★★
A courageous and spirited adventurer with an equally badass sister.

ADRIAN

Will your future son be strong, fearless and have an uncanny ability to punch death relentlessly in the face? If so, why not name him after Britain's unkillable soldier, Adrian Carton de Wiart (b.1880)?

Lieutenant General Sir Adrian Paul Ghislain Carton de Wiart was a British army officer and aristocrat of Belgian and Irish descent. He is famous for surviving at least eleven wounds across three wars, two plane crashes, literally 'calling in the cavalry' by spearheading infantry charges on three continents and tunnelling out of a prisoner of war camp. He was shot in the face three times, and also in the head, stomach, ankle, leg, hip and ear. When a doctor refused outright to amputate Adrian's damaged fingers, he simply tore them off. He lost a hand, an eye and a lung and some reckon that he accumulated enough shrapnel in his body to put the steel industry completely out of business.

BADASS RATING: ★★★★★
Invincible, completely fearless – and probably still alive.

AGNES

Will your girl grow up to be sassy, with steely determination? Will she be bold and brash with brains to boot? Then name her after Lady Agnes Randolph (1312–69), the Scottish woman who pretty much singlehandedly crushed a troop of 20,000 men and saved Dunbar Castle from English rule.

When a swarm of Englishmen had a crack at ambushing her castle, tough-as-nails Agnes fought back like an absolute boss. She hurled giant rocks at approaching enemies, outwitted their attempts at blocking supplies of food and water, set ablaze nearby land and generally laughed off their numerous unsuccessful assaults. After nineteen long weeks of various failed attempts at the siege, the English were broken and beaten into submission and retreated sheepishly home.

BADASS RATING: ★★★★
Rowdy, riotous and an absolute legend.

Agnodice

Will your future daughter be kind, compassionate and smart? Will she be unafraid to strip naked and run through the streets in order to save thousands of lives? Then name her after the Athenian woman who stopped at nothing to help the people: the first ever female physician quite possibly in the history of the universe, Agnodice (*c.* fourth century BC).

Agnodice knew that giving birth in the fourth century BC was pretty dire. The all-male doctors were unsympathetic, a labouring mama's needs were overlooked and death rates were at an all-time high. So she decided she had to help. Women were not allowed to practise medicine, obvs, but Agnodice thought 'screw the patriarchy' and simply donned a pair of trousers, chopped off her hair, renamed herself Augustus and trained as a gynaecologist.

When her sisters discovered she was secretly one of them, they insisted on seeing her for all their gynaecological needs. She delivered a record number of babies and became so popular that the men of Athens started to get suspicious. Of course, they convinced themselves she must have been seducing their wives. So they charged her for it.

Hauled up in a court room and on trial, Agnodice decided there was only one way to deal with the situation. Like a true badass, she tore off all her clothes, revealed her womanhood and danced wildly around the court.

Of course the patriarchy then tried to hang her for masquerading as a man, but when their wives caught wind of this, they rallied for her release. Girl power won and, not only that, the law was changed to enable women to legally study and practise medicine. Result.

BADASS RATING: ★★★★
The physician who smashed the patriarchy!

AGUSTINA

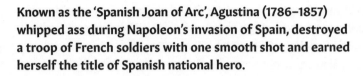

Known as the 'Spanish Joan of Arc', Agustina (1786–1857) whipped ass during Napoleon's invasion of Spain, destroyed a troop of French soldiers with one smooth shot and earned herself the title of Spanish national hero.

When the French military roared into the city of Zaragoza, it is fair to say the Spanish were ill prepared – their only defence being a couple of rusty cannons. Agustina was sent out to deliver a basket of apples to the Spanish soldiers. On approaching the city's walls, she came to an abrupt halt, aghast at the quivering gunman supposedly defending the city. She threw her basket of apples to the ground, launched herself at an abandoned cannon, fired it up and blasted the living shit out of a group of advancing French.

The Spanish soldiers were so in awe that they sprang to their feet and attacked the French with such gusto they were forced to flee the city. Zaragoza was saved!

Agustina was recruited to lead the Spanish army and launched a counter attack against Napoleon. She was captured and imprisoned, but that didn't stop her from wreaking total havoc. She broke out of prison, went undercover for the Spanish *guerrilleros* and raided French army supply bases. When the Brits and Spaniards joined forces, the Duke of Wellington was so in admiration of her fearlessness he appointed her his officer, and together they smashed the French army into submission.

BADASS RATING: ★★★★★
This woman kicked more balls than all the Real Madrid players have in a lifetime.

AIMÉE

Will your daughter be fearless? Will she travel the world on a wild adventure, living a rich and full life? Then name her after Aimée Crocker (1864–1941).

An American gold and railroad heiress, princess and bohemian, Aimée was famous for magnificent and outrageous parties (she once hosted a society dinner wearing nothing more than an enormous boa constrictor), eclectic lovers (a feudal Chinese warlord), adopted children and fabulous tattoos.

On divorcing her first husband, she kissed America goodbye and set off on the nineteenth-century equivalent of a reckless gap year. Aimée dodged wild headhunters in Borneo, survived an attempted poisoning in Hong Kong and avoided being almost murdered in Shanghai.

During her travels through Hawaii, the king was so enchanted by Aimée's lust for life that he declared her a princess and gifted her an island. Aimée also shagged her way through the hypnotists of Honolulu, experienced orgasms via stringed instruments in Beijing and escaped angry tribes in Maasi – her life was one long, exhilarating ride.

BADASS RATING: ★★★★
Hedonistic, naughty and living a life with zero boundaries, Aimee was a total badass!

ALASDAIR

Is your wee bubba going to enter the world as a hellraising gladiator? Will he possess strength and bravery, and go to great lengths to protect his clan? Then name him after Alasdair Mac Colla (1610–47).

Alasdair was a seven-foot, tartan-clad, musket-firing, nuts Scottish Highlander, who developed a great fondness for charging at his enemies in battle (a move now famously known as the 'Highland charge'). When Alasdair's clan were forced out of Scotland by a crew of house-torching, land-thieving rogues called the Campbells, Alasdair was forced to relocate to Ireland.

Once across the Irish Sea, Alasdair set about wreaking revenge on the Campbells for stealing his land. He swiftly recruited an army of over 2,000 Irishmen, trained them up to a standard that would make Braveheart look feeble and charged back into Scotland. Victory after victory in bloody battle eventually led Alasdair to team up with another general, the marquis of Montrose, and together they began a crusade of retribution across the country.

BADASS RATING: ★★★★
A great Celtic badass, famous for his reckless military heroism in the Wars of the Three Kingdoms.

ALBERT

Want your future son to know that life is full of second chances? Then give him the namesake of Britain's most dedicated and longest-serving hangman turned swashbuckling anti-capital punishment activist, Albert Pierrepoint (1905–92).

Born into a long line of hangmen, it was no surprise that Albert took up the ropes, qualifying as chief executioner before the age of twenty. He tried his best to be as humane as possible, and was praised for his quick executions and casual wit. During his career, he hanged more than 600 people, with a record of 17 in a single day. By night he ran a local public house, never speaking of his other job – until one morning when he awoke with a start, questioned the ethics of his career choice and resigned from the Home Office with immediate effect.

With a new sense of morality, he began to fight tirelessly for the end of the death penalty. Not only did Albert feverishly rally against the government's stance on capital punishment, he also pounded out a memoir as a dark warning against the notion of 'an eye for an eye' and moved to the seaside to repent his previous life.

BADASS RATING: ★
Hangman turned capital punishment avenger.

ALBIE

Want to give your future son the namesake of an all-round decent human? Then name him after the death-defying freedom fighter and lawyer Albie Sachs (b.1935).

At the age of seventeen, Albie stuck two fingers up to apartheid by staging a coup in his local post office and deliberately sitting in the area reserved for blacks. He was subsequently arrested, but this small incident marked the beginning of a lifelong campaign for equal rights for all.

Unafraid to speak out against injustice, Albie has been nicked more times than a hotel shampoo bottle. He survived a car bomb in Mozambique that destroyed his right arm and left him blinded in one eye. Despite enduring decades of bullying and harassment for choosing to work as a lawyer representing black defendants, he has relentlessly continued to fight for social justice.

One of his most famous achievements is that, on his appointment to the Constitutional Court of South Africa by Nelson Mandela, he made a landmark ruling that legalized same-sex marriage in South Africa. He has also written a bunch of books exposing the shameless sexism and discrimination against women within the legal system, and has generally tried his damned best to make the world a better place.

BADASS RATING: ★★★★★
A tireless warrior on a mission for equality.

ALEXANDER

How about naming your son after Alexander Hamilton (1755–1804), an all-round American badass and one of the founding fathers of the United States?

Alexander came from humble roots. Growing up in the West Indies, he was orphaned young and forced to leave education to work as a clerk in a trading house. One day he wrote a letter to his local newspaper and the editor was so impressed by his brave and powerful authorship that he raised money to send him to university in America. But Alexander sacked off college to join the revolution, and swiftly became George Washington's most senior aide and all-round fearless wingman.

When the war was over he casually gained entry to the New York bar without any formal legal education, and quickly built a reputation as a banging lawyer who was not afraid to call out bullshit. He co-authored the *Federalist Papers*, founded America's first bank, the Bank of New York, and became the first treasury secretary of the United States – all before the age of thirty. He also fought hard to abolish slavery, championed somewhat controversial ideas for his time and generally kicked ass.

BADASS RATING: ★★★★
A charismatic, self-made leader who helped shape modern-day America.

ALFRED

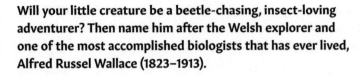

Will your little creature be a beetle-chasing, insect-loving adventurer? Then name him after the Welsh explorer and one of the most accomplished biologists that has ever lived, Alfred Russel Wallace (1823–1913).

Alfred was the kind of kid who was always digging around in soil, dissecting small bugs and going on wild camping trips to get closer to nature. At twenty-five, having exhausted the Welsh countryside of new discoveries, he set sail to Brazil. He bravely crossed the Amazon and collected specimens of insects, birds and any other animal he could find in the tropical rainforest. But on his return to England, his ship caught fire and all his samples and writings were burnt to cinders. Like a total hardass, Alfred spent ten days clinging to a rubber dinghy in ice-cold waters before eventually being rescued. Alfred 1: Death 0.

Undeterred, he set sail for the Malay Archipelago to start his studies again. He travelled over 14,000 miles, collected 110,000 insects, 7,500 shells, 8,050 bird skins and 410 specimens of mammals and reptiles. He then knocked out a ground-breaking paper, which, put simply, attributed the theory of evolution to natural selection. This was way before Darwin had published his own paper with the very same musings.

BADASS RATING: ★★★
The unsung hero who should actually be remembered for developing the theory of evolution.

ALICE

Want to inspire your daughter to break out of the mould? Then name her after the woman who invented the narrative film, Alice Guy-Blaché (1873–1968).

While working as secretary for Léon Gaumont, the founder of the first French motion picture company, Alice borrowed some of the equipment and began filming her own project in her spare time. Until this point the industry had mostly made films for the purpose of science or to sell a camera, but Alice wanted to create something different. She wanted to create stories, and so in 1896, she became the first person ever to direct a fictional film.

From Paris to New York, for over twenty-five years Alice directed, wrote and produced more than a thousand films. She set up and ran her own film studio in New Jersey and is known for her ground-breaking experimentation with sound syncing, colour tinting, interracial casting and special effects.

BADASS RATING: ★★★★
The world's first female film director and boundary-busting badass.

ALLAN

Will your baby possess qualities of determination, righteousness and courage? Then name him after Allan Pinkerton (1819–84), the barrel-making, hard-as-nails Scotsman who moved to America, accidentally fell into a career of crime-busting and went on to become the greatest detective the world has ever seen.

While out hunting for timber one day, Allan stumbled across a bunch of charlatans and decided to keep an eye on their movements. When he tipped off the local sheriff and they were subsequently arrested, everyone was so impressed by this humble act of badassery that Allan was offered the role of the first police detective in Chicago. Despite having zero previous experience, Allan accepted the job and then went on to win 'employee of the decade' by arresting more crooks and killers than anyone else on the force.

For some, this might be enough law-enforcing, villain-smashing greatness, but Allan didn't stop there. He went on to set up the Pinkerton National Detective Agency, which grew to be larger than the US army and created the first ever database of criminals, leading to the birth of the FBI. He famously foiled an assassination attempt on Abraham Lincoln, hunted down Jesse James and Butch Cassidy on horseback, and also had a hand in setting up the secret service.

BADASS RATING: ★★★★
A relentless overachiever who led a fearless crusade of law enforcement.

ALTHEA

Reckon your daughter's going to run before she can walk? How about naming her after the super-skilled boundary-busting athlete, Althea Gibson (1927–2003)?

It took Althea less than a year to go from first picking up a racquet to charging onto the tennis court, delivering a killer serve and playing with such fierce skill that she won a local tournament – thereby earning herself an honourable reputation for mad racquet skills among American tennis's most elite.

A woman of colour from a poor suburb of New York, Althea smashed her way through every prejudice to become the first great African-American player in women's tennis. She was the first black player to compete at Wimbledon, and subsequently the first black player to win the whole tournament. Althea also became the first black player to win the French and US Open titles. A truly inspirational woman, Althea won a total of fifty-six national and international singles and doubles titles, including five Wimbledon trophies.

BADASS RATING: ★★★★
A tour de force who smashed the colour line in international tennis, paving the way for stars of the future.

AMELIA

Will your little boots be a fearless adrenaline junkie? Will she do everything within her power to make her dreams take flight? Then name her after the adventure-loving aviator and wonder woman that was Amelia Earhart (1897–1937).

From building a flight-ramp on the top of her family shed as a little girl to working as a truck driver, stenographer and photographer to pay for lessons, Amelia was determined to soar the skies. She became the first woman ever to fly an aeroplane above 14,000 feet. She was the first woman to fly solo across the Atlantic; the first woman to fly an autogiro; she smashed transatlantic speed records and even set up her own airline company, which still runs commercial flights today.

Defining act of badassery: the time she leaped out of her plane mid-race and ran through the balls of fire bursting out from another aircraft to pull her fellow competitor to safety. Not only did she save a life, Amelia then then hopped back in her cockpit and completed the race, coming in third!

BADASS RATING: ★★★★★
A daring, inspirational, patriarchy-smashing, record-breaking machine.

ANA

Want to name your daughter after a legendary warrior who roared across Peru with her lesbian lover, avenging criminals at the point of her sword? Take inspiration from Ana Lezama de Urinza (born and died sometime in the 1600s).

Orphaned young, Ana grew up on the streets of Potosi, Bolivia (which used to be part of Peru), honing her skills as a tough-as-nails chick. When she became bosom buddies with Eustaquia de Sonza, the daughter of a Potosian aristocrat, she was adopted into her family. Alongside her friend and later her lover, teenage Ana learnt the art of fencing from Peru's most famous sword-master, how to fire a gun and generally all the skills you need to become a teenage tearaway.

Ana and Eustaquia spent many years blazing across Peru on horseback, dressing up as men to enter bars, drinking and following adventure or showing off their blade skills. And when Ana wasn't jousting with her enemies, she was in a ring, taking a bull head-on and fast becoming known as the biggest badass in Potosi.

BADASS RATING: ★★★★
Swordswoman, bull-fighter and the ultimate renegade rebel.

ANGELA

Will your daughter be rich in kindness? Loving and giving with such abundance that she deserves the namesake Angela Burdett Coutts (1814–1906)?

Philanthropist Angela inherited her grandfather's wealth, but instead of kicking back and living the good life, she did everything within her power to help those in need – from creating homes for the poor in east London to building a safe house for young women working the streets. Angela also co-founded the London Society for the Prevention of Cruelty to Children, supported nurses and generally gave help to those suffering in every corner of the globe.

A fearless feminist, Angela shunned the convention of marriage for many years, instead choosing to live with her good friend and former governess. But by her sixties, Angela decided to give married life a whirl and wed a handsome young American forty years her junior. She insisted he take her name in matrimony, and because of a clause in her late father's will prescribing the kind of man she should marry, she had to forfeit her entire fortune as a result. Which of course she did.

BADASS RATING: ★★★
Queen of generosity.

ANNIE

Got a little stuntwoman performing somersaults in your pregnant belly? Then name her after the daredevil dowager who rolled down the Niagara Falls in a pickle barrel, Annie Edson Taylor (1838–1921).

Annie was not your average sixty-three-year-old school teacher. At some point in her later life, she decided her calling was to perform death-defying stunts. Perhaps she thought her antics might draw enough crowds to fund a leisurely retirement in the sun, but whatever the motives, Annie was about to prove some extreme badassery.

First she tested her stunt out on her cat. She launched the unsuspecting mog over the edge of the world's deadliest waterfall in a sealed barrel. When he came back bewildered, slightly bruised but otherwise still breathing, Annie knew it was her time to shine. In 1901 she became the first nutter to survive dropping down the Niagara Falls – 53 metres of cascading water. Annie made her descent in a sealed barrel, vowing afterwards that she would rather stick her head in a cannon than ever do it again. It has been reported that a few years later she became the first nutter to survive rolling over the edge of the falls a second time. There was no end to Annie's brave insanity.

BADASS RATING: ★★★
A brave, bat-shit crazy kinda badass.

ARISTOTLE

Does the fuzzy lanugo-covered newborn snuggling in your arms look pensive? Perhaps his future calling will be the study of philosophy? Then name him after the greatest thinker to have ever lived, Aristotle (384–322 BC).

With a bottomless brain of burgeoning brilliance, Aristotle was an A1 badass of the highest order. Lots of smart people regard him as the hot-shot who knew everything there was to know – the biggest mastermind to have ever walked the earth, which is a pretty banging endorsement. Plato called him 'the Mind', which is apt, as he was a scholar in physics, medicine, geology, metaphysics, poetry, politics, history, government, ethics and basically every subject in the world.

With thoughts running faster than Usain Bolt after five flat whites and half a gram of speed, it is no surprise that Aristotle made significant discoveries in almost every walk of life. He invented formal logic, psychology, descriptive biology and a heap of other things. His principles of ethics are still taught today – he encouraged acts of kindness, self-care before it was even a trending hashtag and was an all-round first-rate human being.

BADASS RATING: ★ ★ ★ ★
Whatever anyone is thinking right now, Aristotle probably already thought it.

ARTHUR

Do the little kicks from your future son feel like those of a renegade rebel? A daring double-agent with more sauce than 007? Then name him after Arthur Owens (1899–1957).

An unsuccessful Welsh battery inventor turned Second World War spy, Arthur fooled the Germans into hiring him as their secret weapon when he had already deceptively taken up a post at MI5. Code-named Snow by British intelligence, Arthur was the balls and the brains behind the Double Cross system and responsible for busting over 120 Nazi moles, forcing them to work undercover for the Brits and send false information back to the Jerries. A cool-headed sleuth, he was also part of the squad that duped Hitler over the location of the D-Day landings and saved the lives of thousands of Allies. What a guy!

BADASS RATING: ★★★
A man of mystery with a legendary role in helping the Allies win the war.

MORE AWESOME As

ADELA

Adela Pankhurst (1885–1961) was a ball-busting, awe-inspiring suffragette who snuck over to Australia to smash up the patriarchy down under and wage a war against inequality.

BADASS RATING: ★★★★

AMERIGO

Amerigo Vespucci (1454–1512) was a Florentine explorer who sailed across the oceans, discovered Rio de Janeiro and became the namesake for an entire continent – America.

BADASS RATING: ★★★

AMINA

Amina of Zaria (1533–*c.*1610) was a hard-as-nails Hausa warrior queen who tore her way across north Nigeria, expanding her kingdom at breakneck speed. She shunned the life of marriage, instead choosing to take on a temporary lover after each victorious battle.

BADASS RATING: ★★★

MORE AWESOME As

AMY

Amy Winehouse (1983–2011) was the beautiful, gravel-voiced singer who won a bunch of Grammys and sold over five million records in a ridiculously short amount of time. Amy created a musical legacy that will live forever.

BADASS RATING: ★★★★

ANN

Ann Bonny (*c.*1697–*c.*1782) was a flame-haired, hot-blooded, ball-breaking Irish pirate who owned the Caribbean seas in the eighteenth century.

BADASS RATING: ★★★★

ANTOINETTE

Antoinette Brown Blackwell (1825–1921) was an outspoken women's rights crusader and powerhouse who became the first woman to be ordained a Protestant minister in the United States.

BADASS RATING: ★★★★

MORE AWESOME As

APHRA

Aphra Behn (1640–89) was the first woman in British history to earn a living from her writing. Aphra blazed her way through cultural barriers to become an icon and literary role model.

BADASS RATING: ★ ★ ★ ★

ARNOLD

Arnold Alois Schwarzenegger (b.1947) is a tank-owning, bodybuilding self-made millionaire and 'governator' of California who created some of the most badass scenes in film history.

BADASS RATING: ★ ★ ★

ASTRID

Astrid Lindgren (1907–2002) was a Swedish writer, activist and creator of the beloved Pippi Longstocking – one of the first inspirational female characters in children's literature, known for her strength, independence and general badassery.

BADASS RATING: ★ ★ ★

MORE AWESOME As

ATWOOD

Margaret Atwood (b.1939) is the legendary Booker Prize-winning Canadian poet and novelist who has created many works of genius, including *The Handmaid's Tale*.

BADASS RATING: ★★★★★

AUDRE

Audre Lorde (1934–92) was a pimpin' poet, feminist and civil rights campaigner who implored all minorities to speak out and break the silence of oppression.

BADASS RATING: ★★★★

BARACK

The baby boy in your belly is going to fill your lives with so much happiness, so why not give him a moniker to be proud of: name him after the biggest badass in US presidential history, Barack Obama (b.1961).

Barack ended the war in Iraq, introduced affordable healthcare into America and reduced unemployment rates. He has fearlessly campaigned against climate change and cut greenhouse gas emissions in the US. He legalized same-sex marriages in the US, championed equal pay, doubled the number of female justices in Supreme Court history and led the operation to take out Osama bin Laden. No wonder he was awarded the Nobel Peace Prize after only nine months in the Oval Office.

He also real-life dropped the mic as he signed out of the White House. #lifegoals

BADASS RATING: ★★★★★
A president with swagger who transformed America.

BARBARA

Will your future daughter use her energy and generosity to make the world a fairer place? Take inspiration from the artist, feminist, women's liberationist and law reformer, Barbara Leigh Smith Bodichon (1827–91).

A fearless crusader for women's equality, Barbara waged a war against the establishment to promote a woman's right to education, to vote and to work.

Her upbringing was unconventional, as her father treated all his children as equals, no matter their sex. Empowered by unusual wealth and freedom, Barbara used her money to co-fund the opening of Girton College in Cambridge, the first university to offer women education to degree level.

Barbara was frank and unapologetic. She set up the *English Women's Journal* and formed the first ever Women's Suffrage Committee and spent her life fighting against the legal restrictions under which women lived. She wrote world-changing papers on this subject, as well as books, journals and pamphlets. She sought to change the legal rights of married women and took her campaign to the House of Commons, where she gave evidence to a fearsome committee. It is largely thanks to Barbara's awe-inspiring badassery that in 1857 an act was passed protecting the property rights of divorced women. Down with the patriarchy!

BADASS RATING: ★★★★
One of the most influential leaders of the Victorian women's movement.

BARNARDO

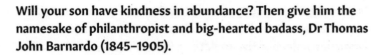

Will your son have kindness in abundance? Then give him the namesake of philanthropist and big-hearted badass, Dr Thomas John Barnardo (1845–1905).

Irish-born Barnardo moved to London to train as a doctor, but was so moved by the devastating effects of poverty he saw in the East End that he immediately abandoned his studies and began a mission to help those in need. He took to the streets, preached on pub corners and rallied enough funds to open a safe house for destitute children.

Following his first house in Stepney Causeway, he built 95 more homes, which cared for over 8,500 children. And in his lifetime, it is believed Barnardo rescued almost 60,000 children from poverty and assisted more than 250,000 children in some way.

His philosophy was simple: every child deserves the best possible start in life – and he made damn sure he did all that he could to make this happen.

BADASS RATING: ★★★★★
A hero who radicalized the way Victorians responded to poverty and created a legacy that continues to help those in need.

BARTHOLOMEW

Is the baby in your belly already boss? Will he be brazen, smart as fuck, invincible and possess all the badass qualities to command a fleet of five hundred pirates? Then name him after the legendary buccaneer and ruler of the seas, Bartholomew Roberts (1682–1722).

A hornswaggling, shanty-singing Welshman, Bartholomew was known for his fine dress sense, womanizing and expert plundering skills. Hailed as the most notorious pirate of the Golden Age, he captured and looted over four hundred vessels in just three short years and headed up a fleet of four ass-kicking pillaging machines.

He may have charged across the waters between America and Africa, scuttling any ships that lay in his path and leaving a trail of destruction, but Bartholomew also set up some pretty awesome rules of piracy. He went out of his way to ensure all his crew had equal rights – whether it was voting on ship affairs, access to fresh food or the division of loot.

BADASS RATING: ★★★★
The most successful and dangerous pirate to ever sail the high seas.

BAYARD

Will your little bean grow into a calm, cool and all-round decent human, who is not afraid to stand by his beliefs? Then name him after the civil rights activist and Martin Luther King's esteemed advisor, Bayard Rustin (1912–87).

An avid promoter of non-violence, Bayard was a damn good organizer of human rights protests. As a young black gay activist, he was often arrested because of his own civil disobedience, but no amount of time behind bars would stop him from being true to his badass self and he continued to be openly homosexual.

Bayard was the powerhouse behind the march in Aldermaston, England where 10,000 protesters made a stand against nuclear warfare. He was the inspiration for Martin Luther King to give up using guns to defend his home and instead promote Gandhi's philosophy of non-violent resistance. He stood up against racial segregation and calmly championed gay rights.

Once, during a protest, a stranger started attacking Bayard with a stick. Rather than respond with an eye for an eye or attempt an escape, Bayard simply picked up another stick, handed it over to his assailant and then casually asked him if he fancied beating him with that one too.

BADASS RATING: ★★★
A brave and confident pacifist who tried to make the world a better place.

BEAR

Will your future son be the ultimate survivalist? Then name him after the bat-shit crazy adventurer, Bear Grylls (b.1974).

Resourceful and with nerves of steel, Bear has swum with crocodiles, hosted a dinner party at 24,262 feet, rowed butt-naked along the Thames in a bathtub for 22 miles, broken records as the youngest person to climb to the tip of Mount Everest (just 18 months after smashing up three of his vertebrae during a disastrous parachute jump) and has dived head-first into quicksand just for the hell of it.

An SAS expert, Bear is trained in parachute jumping, unarmed combat and jungle warfare and has merrily thrown himself into a ton of life-threatening situations in order to make good TV.

The man will also consume anything. From chowing down on camel dung, poisonous spiders, yak eyeballs and lava beetles to drinking his own piss – if he can fit it in his mouth, he'll eat it.

BADASS RATING: ★★★★
Apparently the youngest ever chief scout and a man with NO FEAR.

Beate

Want a sure-fire way to broach the subject of practising safe sex with your future daughter? Give her the name Beate, after the aeronautical daredevil who pioneered sexual education in Germany while simultaneously opening the world's very first sex shop – Beate Uhse (1919–2001).

Beate was a trained stunt pilot – the first ever woman in Germany to qualify – but because of her involvement with the Luftwaffe, at the end of the Second World War, she was banned from ever flying again. With her husband dead, a young son to support and dreams of soaring the skies abandoned, Beate made ends meet working on the black market selling a range of products with the casual friendliness of an unauthorized door-to-door Avon sales rep.

On her rounds she met women whose husbands had returned home and put a bun in the oven; afraid of the extra mouth to feed, they turned to backstreet abortions, sometimes with grave consequences. Given Beate's mother had been pretty savvy at dishing out the sex ed. to her daughter, Beate decided to create a marriage guide for women. It was adorned with tips and tricks on the best days to conceive and also how to avoid unwanted pregnancy, and was a roaring success. Beate then took her company to the heady heights of mail-order condoms before opening a chain of saucy shops that spread across Europe.

BADASS RATING: ★★★
A renowned advocate for safe sex and champion of women's reproductive rights.

BELLE

Will your girl be dauntless and carefree with the gift of the gab? Then take inspiration from Belle Boyd (1844–1900), a Civil War spy turned author and actor and all-round tough nut.

Belle's espionage career began by total accident when she became so infuriated by a Union soldier who dared to curse at her mother that she reached for the nearest gun and promptly shot and killed him. She was just seventeen at the time, but her brazen behaviour caught the eye of the Confederate army and she became one of their official spies.

Blessed with charm, Belle was known to flirt outrageously with soldiers while sneakily extracting information from them to pass on to the opposition. Her early missions often involved racing across battlefields, ducking heavy fire, to deliver vital information and supplies to Southern troops. She was regularly arrested and was eventually banished to England, where she fell in love with a Union officer and controversially married him!

Belle became an actor later in life, tragically dying on stage during a live performance.

BADASS RATING: ★
The nineteenth century's most sassy spy.

BELVA

Will your teeny tot have a thirst for knowledge? Then name her after the boundary-busting badass who raised the bar, Belva Ann Lockwood (1830–1917).

Widowed and a single mother at just twenty-two, Belva used the little money her husband had left her to follow her dreams of education. With steely determination and while working on the side to pay the bills, Belva went to college and then university, travelling across America to fulfil her desires.

As a woman she faced a lot of discrimination, but Belva was not about to take any bullshit. Noticing that men doing equal work to her were paid more, she lobbied for an equal pay act in federal government. And won.

After completing her studies in law she was denied a degree based on her gender, so she appealed directly to the president. She won again. Once qualified, she discovered that female lawyers were not allowed to argue before the Supreme Court, so guess what Belva did? She rallied to pass legislation that allowed women to do so and, of course, she won.

BADASS RATING: ★★★★
The lawyer pioneer who refused to take 'no' for an answer.

Bernadette

Want to inspire your daughter to stand up for herself and others? Then give her the namesake Bernadette, after the totally radical Irish MP, Bernadette Devlin (b.1947).

When the Conservative home secretary argued in parliament that the British army had shot dead thirteen unarmed activists in 'self defence' on what is now known as Bloody Sunday, Bernadette did one of the most badass things any MP has done in history. She stood up, crossed the floor of the House of Commons and punched Reginald Maudling in the face. The year was 1972 and Bernadette was just twenty-one years old. We salute you, Bernadette!

BADASS RATING: ★★★★★
Feminist, human rights campaigner and the youngest woman ever elected to parliament in 1969.

BERYL

Will your future daughter be bold, brave and ambitious? Will she reach for the sky and fearlessly follow her dreams? Then name her after aviator pioneer, racehorse trainer, author and adventurer, Beryl Markham (1902–1986).

Beryl was the first woman in Africa (and quite probably the world) to get a racehorse trainer's licence. All before she had even celebrated her nineteenth birthday. An affair with British pilot Tom Campbell Black inspired her to retrain as an aviator and she became the first woman in Africa to get her professional licence. From bush pilot to record-breaker: Beryl was the first woman to fly solo across the Atlantic 'the hard way' – from east to west, flying blindly through atrocious weather and eventually crash landing in a bog in Nova Scotia. Not bad for someone who was apparently kicked out of school for being a prankster.

Beryl also wrote a bestselling memoir, *West with the Night*, hailed by Hemingway as 'bloody wonderful'.

BADASS RATING: ★★★
A woman who refused to conform to the expectations of her time, and instead fearlessly followed her dreams.

BESSIE

Feel like your baby is already performing daring loop-the-loops, barrel rolls and figures of eight in your womb? Then take inspiration from the breathtaking stuntwoman and pilot, Bessie Coleman (1892–1926).

Bessie smashed through all gender and racial barriers by becoming the first black woman to hold an international aviation licence. When American piloting schools denied her entry based on her ethnicity, she simply saved up, learnt French and moved to Paris to study the art of flying.

Legendary for her exhilarating aerial manoeuvres, Bessie loved parachuting out of planes, performing near-ground dips and generally dazzling crowds with her sky-soaring skills. She was known to be a no-bullshit, straight-talking thrill-seeker and is often referred to as the world's greatest female flyer.

BADASS RATING: ★★★★
The kind of hardass who died by falling 2,000 feet out of an aeroplane, shortly before it burst into flames.

Betty

Want to teach your future daughter that with hard work, determination and a dose of badassery, she can achieve the impossible? Then look no further than Betty Robinson (1911–99), the athlete left for dead who came back to win gold.

A rising star, Betty was the first American woman to win the 100m sprint at the Olympics, as well as smashed numerous speed records on the track.

At the peak of her career, she was involved in a fatal plane crash and assumed dead. It was only when the undertaker took her body away that he realized there had been a terrible mistake. In a coma for seven months and a wheelchair for six, Betty was not going to let this minor setback stop her career. She learnt to walk again, to run again and built up the strength she once had as a professional athlete. After months and months of endurance and hard training, Betty came back to the track and won gold in the 4x100m relay at the Berlin Olympics. What a woman!

BADASS RATING: ★★★★
Brave and courageous, Betty showed the world just what can be achieved with grit and perseverance.

BIBI

Will your daughter be generous and giving with a side-serving of culinary excellence? Then name her after the Sikh legend who made it her mission to ensure her entire community was nourished, Bibi Khivi (1506–82).

Married to the second Sikh guru, Bibi established a free kitchen to provide meals for those in need. The first to serve Langar, now a long-established Sikh tradition to provide everyone with food, Bibi broke convention to lead her venture. She insisted on working side by side with men and was an early pioneer for female independence. From sweet treats to hearty feasts of nutritious dishes, Bibi sought to provide for all.

BADASS RATING: ★★★★
Bibi smashed through the gender barriers of her time with her enormous generosity.

BILLIE

Are you ready to birth a daughter so badass she will not only become one of the greatest sporting heroes of all time, but will also publicly kick the asses of loud, arrogant chauvinists in honour of the sisterhood? Then give her the namesake Billie Jean King (b.1943).

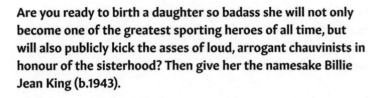

Billie is a former world number 1 tennis player with 39 Grand Slam wins to her name; she won Wimbledon 20 times and is a fearless pioneer for equality. Billie famously took on Bobby Riggs in a match dubbed by the media as the 'Battle of the Sexes'. Bobby was so confident he would win that he whipped the world into a pre-match frenzy by mocking Billie and essentially attempting to shame the entire female population. So Billie did what any true rebel would do – she strode onto the court and absolutely destroyed him.

BADASS RATING: ★★★★
Icon, legend and tennis superstar.

BLAS

Growing a ball of fire? Can you feel your little life barnacle's fierce determination to keep battling on like no other man and deliver a giant victorious punch to the face of adversity? Then name him after Don Blas de Lezo (1689–1741).

Blas was the Spanish navy's greatest hero, a one-legged, one-eyed and one-armed powerhouse who refused to quit in battle, even when the odds were stacked so high against his crew, enemies were celebrating victories before fighting had even ceased.

When the Brits attacked the city of Cartagena in 1741, the Spanish were outnumbered eight to one. Many of their vessels were seriously damaged or had been captured in early attacks, but Admiral Blas was not about to surrender. He instead launched an attack on the British fleet in the dead of night and this shrewd act of badassery went on to save the city from their rule. Blas' statue now stands in front of Castillo San Felipe de Barajas as an acknowledgement that he is one of the Spanish navy's great strategists.

BADASS RATING: ★★★★
Nothing will stop this ninja from protecting his city.

BLENDA

Want to name your little button after the feisty Swedish beauty who fought off an army of Danes with a kickass squad of women? Then call her Blenda, who lived at some point between the sixth and eighth centuries AD.

Instead of wielding axes and charging into battle, Blenda had the cunning idea of getting her crew of Viking-slaying vixens to simply slide up to the Danish soldiers and shower them with flattery. This worked pretty well and the Danes paused their attack, deciding it would be a cool idea to host a party for everyone to feast and enjoy some fine wine together. A fatal mistake on their part. When the Danish soldiers fell into a deep sleep after a few too many sherries, Blenda and her band of sisters killed them all.

The king of Sweden was so impressed by Blenda's slick victory that he changed a whole bunch of rules to give women equal rights to men.

BADASS RATING: ★ ★ ★ ★
Sassy, smart and brave – don't mess with Blenda.

BOUDICA

Want to teach your daughter to be strong, independent and to not take any shit? Then give her the namesake Boudica (*c*.20–60 AD, although totally unknown) – the warrior-queen famous for showing the Romans who was boss.

After her husband, Boudica was next in line to the throne of British tribe the Iceni. But when he died and the Romans refused to acknowledge her as queen, Boudica was furious. (It didn't help that they were total a**holes who had also raped her two daughters.) And so she gathered an army of over 200,000 soldiers and charged into the neighbouring city, which we now know as Colchester, fire-balling Roman temples and killing almost 70,000 civilians. She then burnt London to the ground, seriously freaking out the Romans, who withdrew almost all forces from Britain as a result.

BADASS RATING: ★★★★★
A tough-as-nails queen who has become a national hero and symbol of freedom.

BUZZ

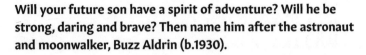

Will your future son have a spirit of adventure? Will he be strong, daring and brave? Then name him after the astronaut and moonwalker, Buzz Aldrin (b.1930).

First, Buzz roared across the skies as a fighter pilot in the Korean War. After surviving a mere sixty-six combat missions, he was awarded a Distinguished Flying Cross for his bravery.

When the war was over he studied for a PhD in astronautics, then went to work for NASA, where he really honed being freaking awesome. His first assignment was to spacewalk as part of the Gemini 12 crew. He nailed it. Buzz floated around in the deadly vacuum of space for five and a half hours – smashing all the records for the longest spacewalk in history.

In 1969 he made history again, but this time as the pilot of the Apollo 11 mission, where he became the second person to ever step foot on the moon.

Aside from blasting off to outta space on various adventures, Buzz also knocked out a couple of sci-fi bestsellers, recorded a rap with Snoop Dog and famously punched a man in the face when he claimed that the moon landing was a hoax.

BADASS RATING: ★★★★★
Quite possibly the coolest man to walk the earth. AND THE MOON.

MORE BANGING Bs

BASS

Bass Reeves (1838–1910) fled slavery to become one of the most successful lawmen of the American West – known for bringing down entire gangs and arresting over 3,000 criminals.

BADASS RATING: ★★★

BEATE

Beate Gordon (1923–2012) was the woman who empowered and liberated generations of Japanese women by writing their rights into the constitution of modern Japan. A celebrated Japanese icon who changed the world – and all before her twenty-third birthday.

BADASS RATING: ★★★★

BEATRICE

Beatrice Webb (1858–1943) was a brave rebel who devoted herself to the abolition of workhouses. Beatrice was a trailblazer of the Independent Labour Party, and one of the founders of the London School of Economics.

BADASS RATING: ★★★★

MORE BANGING Bs

BETTE

Bette Nesmith Graham (1924–80) was a slick entrepreneur and original inventor of what we now call Tipp-Ex.

BADASS RATING: ★★

BEYONCÉ

Beyoncé Knowles (b.1981) is a singer, songwriter and the most awarded artist in history, who continues to inspire generations of girls to be independent, 100 per cent bona fide badasses.

BADASS RATING: ★★★★★

BILL

Bill McKibben (b.1960) is an environmentalist, activist, author, earth-warrior and pioneer of the biggest global movement against climate change.

BADASS RATING: ★★★

MORE BANGING Bs

BILQUIS

Bilquis (a long time ago) was the actual queen of Sheba! Bilquis rocked across Jerusalem in a caravan filled with spices, gold and other precious trinkets to give King Solomon a good grilling.

BADASS RATING: ★ ★ ★ ★

BIRD

Bird Millman (1890–1940) was a circus performer extraordinaire who dazzled audiences with her derring-do by walking on tightropes suspended over 40 metres (130 feet) above the ground.

BADASS RATING: ★ ★ ★

BLAINE

David Blaine (b.1973) is the hardcore, bat-shit crazy magician whose numerous stunts include starving himself for forty-four days, holding his breath for over seventeen minutes and freezing himself into a block of ice for seventy-two hours – all just for funsies.

BADASS RATING: ★ ★ ★ ★

MORE BANGING Bs

BLANDINA

Blandina Segale (1850–1941) was a nineteenth-century nun who singlehandedly stopped infamous outlaw Billy the Kid from murdering four doctors.

BADASS RATING: ★★★★★

BLAZE

Blaze Starr (1932–2015), known as 'The Hottest Blaze in Burlesque', was a dare-devil dancer who performed with panthers and was often literally on fire. A feminist, businesswoman and property tycoon, Blaze was sassy AF.

BADASS RATING: ★★★

BLYTHE

Blythe Daley (1901–65) was a ball-breaking Broadway actor, better known for her bisexuality, famous friendships and for giving zero fucks.

BADASS RATING: ★

MORE BANGING Bs

BRIGITTE

Brigitte Bardot (b.1934), the outrageous and outspoken screen goddess who walked out on acting to become a fierce and frank animal rights campaigner.

BADASS RATING: ★★

BYRON

George Gordon Byron, aka Lord Byron (1788–1824), was the greatest poet of the Romantic era, a talented and flamboyant man who smoked and shagged and drank his way through life, perfecting the art of giving zero fucks.

BADASS RATING: ★★

Campbell

Will your future son be warm-hearted and selfless with generosity in abundance? Then name him after the benevolent bear-making wonder boy who created an empire of kindness, Campbell Remess (b.2004).

Campbell's motto is simple: 'Everyone can do something.' When he was just nine years old, armed with some freshly sharpened scissors, his mother's old machine and a desperate wish to do something to help those in need, he made the very first bear of kindness. It was a scruffy little rag and took over forty hours of blood, sweat and hard graft, but Campbell wrapped it up and sent it to a child who was undergoing chemotherapy in the hope of bringing a small piece of cheer. He then sat back down at his sewing machine and spent the next few years bashing out a production line of wonder bears that would make Hasbro look like a bunch of amateurs.

From Paris to Pakistan, Campbell gifted his bears to those in need across the world. With his super teds auctioning off for over $5,000 each, he raised such a colossal amount of cash that he was able to set up a new wing of his charity offering Kindness Cruises to those with terminal illness. What an awesome human being, whose simple acts of kindness are enough to make you permanently moist in the eye!

BADASS RATING: ★★★★★
Changing the world one bear at a time.

CANTONA

Do those little kicks in your belly belong to a future footballer, perhaps? Then name him after the game's most notorious badass, the high-kicking French forward Eric Cantona (b.1966).

During a particularly emotional match at Crystal Palace, Cantona received a red card for his behaviour on the pitch. As he began the walk of shame towards the touchline, an angry fan in the crowd blasted a tirade of abuse. Now Cantona was more than used to being a verbal punchbag for football fans, but on this particular occasion he was having none of it. He leaped across the barriers and delivered an almighty kung fu kick to the unsuspecting supporter.

Many years later, when Cantona was asked what his greatest kick in footballing history was, he casually replied, 'The one where I kicked that hooligan.'

BADASS RATING: ★
One of the greatest strikers in the world. And not just on the pitch.*

*NB: We do not condone this sort of violence.

CARL

Will your little cub grow up to possess lion-like courage? Will he be ultra-tough, adventurous and have balls of steel? Then name him after the man who has survived elephant stampedes and rhino attacks; who once snaked his way through crocodile-infested waters on an animal carcass and lived to tell the tale; and who famously fought and then killed a leopard with his own bare hands. Yes, that's the taxidermy pioneer and conservationist, Carl Akeley (1864–1926).

While out on a hunting trip in Somaliland, Carl spotted something in tall grass. At first he mistook the lurking leopard for a warthog, but it soon became apparent that this animal was up for some breakfast, and the American adventurer was on the menu. He tried to shoot it but rather unluckily ran out of bullets after the third shot. Instead of cowering in the bushes awaiting his fate on the inside of a wild cat, he took on the leopard bare-handed, eventually ramming his right arm down its throat and strangling it with his single left hand.

BADASS RATING: ★★★★★
The guy who punched death in the face without registering an ounce of fear.

CAROLINE

Do you dream of a daughter who's high-spirited and doggedly determined, hopelessly charming but with a quick tongue? Then take inspiration from the English powerhouse who fought for – and won – rights for married women: Caroline Norton (1808–77).

Married off at nineteen, Caroline refused to be the traditional wife. Resisting the control of her allegedly cruel husband, she instead forged her own path and gained recognition as a much-respected poet and songwriter. One day her husband decided to accuse her and the then prime minister Lord Melbourne of adultery. The trial was laughed out of court, but, in a fit of rage, Caroline's husband denied her access to her three sons, burnt all her work and seized all her possessions – as he could under Victorian matrimonial law. Caroline had no legal rights. So the only thing for a badass like her to do was to start a campaign to change this.

She helped write the Infant Custody Act (1839) and influenced the Matrimonial Causes (Divorce) Act (1857) and the Married Women's Property Act (1870), which gave women separate legal identities. What a total boss!

BADASS RATING: ★★★★
Caroline smashed the patriarchy, giving rights to married women for the first time.

CATERINA

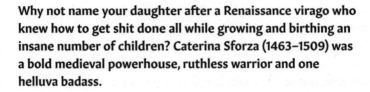
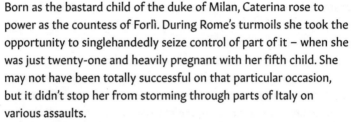

Why not name your daughter after a Renaissance virago who knew how to get shit done all while growing and birthing an insane number of children? Caterina Sforza (1463–1509) was a bold medieval powerhouse, ruthless warrior and one helluva badass.

Born as the bastard child of the duke of Milan, Caterina rose to power as the countess of Forlì. During Rome's turmoils she took the opportunity to singlehandedly seize control of part of it – when she was just twenty-one and heavily pregnant with her fifth child. She may not have been totally successful on that particular occasion, but it didn't stop her from storming through parts of Italy on various assaults.

When her husband was assassinated, Caterina and her children were taken prisoners. The Orsis family was hell-bent on overthrowing her, but this badass was having absolutely none of it. Leaving her children as hostages, Caterina talked her way into an impenetrable fortress and, once inside, turned on her enemies and swore vengeance. They threatened to kill her children, at which point Caterina pulled up her skirt, flashed her privates and bellowed, 'Do it, if you want to! Here I have the instruments to make many more, you bastards!' She eventually took down the enemy troops and regained control of her territory.

BADASS RATING: ★★★
A strong and shrewd military commander, warrior-woman and ball of fire who became a national hero.

CATHERINE

Reckon your girl's gonna rule the world? Right – so name her after the smart, rebellious and powerful Russian empress, Catherine the Great (1729–96).

Catherine realized her husband had questionable leadership potential, so staged a coup against him, kicked him to the kerb and became ruler of Russia. She was notorious for spearheading the expansion of the Russian empire as well as driving political and social reform. As leader, she established the first institutes for education for women in Russia, too. Her self-proclaimed 'gluttony' for art saw her become a patron of the arts and literature and curate one of the world's most impressive art collections in St Petersburg.

Throughout her reign, Catherine enjoyed many lovers and was known to reward a good performance by bestowing a piece of land or a grand title on her conquests.

BADASS RATING: ★★★★
The woman who kicked ass as the longest-ruling female leader of Russia.

CHARLES

Will your son grow up with a nonchalant, no-fear stance towards danger? Then name him after the insane, tightrope-walking French daredevil, Charles Blondin (1824–97).

A fearless and highly skilled acrobat, Charles Blondin made history in 1859 by crossing the Niagara Falls on a 1,300-foot rope, not forgetting to stop every so often to casually take a swig from a bottle of red wine. He later repeated this feat, crossing between the American and Canadian falls on stilts, then proceeded to really hone his stunting badassery with even more outrageous and deadly flair: he once crossed the falls with a sack completely covering his head; then there was the time he did it with his legs locked in chains; another time he crossed the falls pushing a wheelbarrow while giving a piggyback to his equally insane manager. And his *pièce de résistance* was the time he sauntered across the water on a hemp rope carrying a hefty weighted cooking stove, whereupon he stopped halfway, almost 50 metres (150 ft) above cascading water, and whipped up an omelette. As you do.

BADASS RATING: ★★★★★
A man with more daring in his right testicle than most people have in their entire body.

Charlotte

Will your little tootsie be strong and stout-hearted? Then take inspiration from the boundary-busting buccaneer and cut-throat captain, Charlotte de Berry (b.1636).

By disguising herself as a man and sneaking onto a local sailing boat, Charlotte was able to trade a mundane life with a distinctly average family in England to one at the helm of a pirate ship, roaring across the vast oceans. Famous for beheading any sea jackass who tried to force her hand in marriage (of which there were many), any over-attentive male was forced to walk the plank. Eventually Charlotte fell for a Spanish sea rover, but when he was consumed by a shipwrecked crew of ravenous marauders, she jumped to her death, Romeo and Juliet style.

BADASS RATING: ★★★★
A rip-roaring plunder and sailor queen who was always poised to punch the patriarchy – right in the nuts.

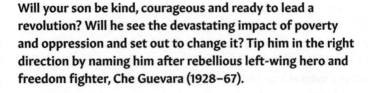

CHE

Will your son be kind, courageous and ready to lead a revolution? Will he see the devastating impact of poverty and oppression and set out to change it? Tip him in the right direction by naming him after rebellious left-wing hero and freedom fighter, Che Guevara (1928–67).

A guerrilla leader, anti-establishment activist and leather-clad, motorbike-riding badass who fought to free Cuba from the clutches of the Batista government and won, Che also served as president of the National Bank of Cuba, told the United States where to go, wrote a bestselling memoir and trained Congolese rebel forces in the art of guerrilla warfare.

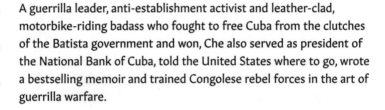

BADASS RATING: ★★★★★
The ultimate anti-capitalist badass and poster boy of rebellion (still adorning the walls of all student accommodation across the land).

CHING

Hey baby-grower, can you feel your little treasure fist-pumping her way to becoming a fearless leader, shrewd businesswoman and ball-breaker who refuses to take any shit? Well, she'll be like Ching Shih (*c.*1770–1844), who wreaked havoc on the oceans assembling and running one of the most kickass pirate armadas in the world.

It all started with marriage to pirate commander Cheng I. As his new wife, Ching Shih gave patriarchy the bunch of fives by demanding equal pay and equal say in her husband's business. Now, if you are going to be a pirate, you may as well be the most successful pirate in history. Together, husband and wife scuttled many ships along the Chinese coastline and grew rich on plunder. When her husband died, Ching was not afraid to take a battleaxe to the heads of those who compromised her or her squad. She valiantly built her fleet to over 300* ships and rarely lost a battle.

BADASS RATING: ★★★★★
Tough and well respected, who can't love a woman who ruled the seas in command of 17,000* men?

*There or thereabouts.

Clara

As the sonographer counts your baby's little fingers during ultrasound, do you imagine them delicately running over the keys of a piano in light lyrical legato? Then perhaps you should consider naming her after one of the most renowned pianists of the Romantic era, the legendary Clara Schumann (1819–96).

A piano prodigy and musical rebel, Clara was playing professionally by the age of nine and touring with large-scale concerts by the time she was twelve. She defied her father by marrying for love and birthed seven children – all while maintaining an esteemed career as a performer and composer because she was a total powerhouse. She shagged whomever she damn well liked, famously corrupting a young Johannes Brahms. Committed, passionate and unafraid to push the boundaries of music, Clara continued to perform across the world with her soulful and distinctive style right up until the day she died.

BADASS RATING: ★★
Skills, sass and one of the greatest piano players of all time.

Coco

Will your future daughter to be ready to break all the rules? Then give her the namesake of the daring designer, businesswoman and awe-inspiring badass, Gabrielle Coco Chanel (1883–1971).

Born in a poorhouse and then orphaned at a young age, Coco was a mostly self-taught seamstress who went from making cabaret costumes to a brief career in millinery before setting up, quite possibly, the coolest clothing empire in the world. And all before she was thirty years old.

Coco ran riot in the world of fashion – she shunned convention and liberated women from corsets, long skirts, crap haircuts and dowdy dresses. She successfully flirted her way to getting business investors. She encouraged women to wear trousers and dialled up the fun in fashion. She also managed to invent a perfume so damn good that it is still bought every thirty seconds today. Coco wreaked havoc in an industry dominated by men and achieved the impossible with glamour, sass and an abundance of badassery.

BADASS RATING: ★★★★★
A true icon and rebel who rewrote the rule book and changed the way we dress forever.

CONNIE

Is baby moving so much you're starting to think you have a tiny circus of aerial gymnasts performing Cirque du Soleil in your womb? Then name her after actor, author, literary agent and all-round mover and shaker, Connie Clausen (1923–97).

She was a badass who ran away to join the circus aged seventeen, rode elephants and horses, then left, wrote a bestselling memoir about circus life and moved on to act on Broadway and television.

But starring in Coca-Cola adverts was not enough and at forty-seven, Connie began a new career in publishing. Quickly rising to vice-president of Macmillan and helping to introduce the world to Richard Adams' *Watership Down* to boot, Connie went on to launch her own literary agency, rocketing the careers of many bestselling authors, including the iconic Quentin Crisp (another great badass right there). What a powerhouse!

BADASS RATING: ★★★
A woman of action – fearless and smart.

CONSTANCE

Will your baby be courageous, brave and strong? So name her after almighty woman and badass Irish freedom fighter, Constance Markievicz (1868–1927).

Constance shunned the life of a socialite, flipped the bird to convention and, instead of getting married young and becoming a dutiful wife, she went to art school, championed socialism and subsequently aided a movement to free Ireland from British rule. When Constance did eventually wed Count Casimir Markievicz, she omitted the part about 'obeying thy husband'. Fuck that.

Once married and with child, Constance was not one for sitting at home knitting tea cosies or batch-cooking jam. Instead she took to the streets of Ireland, delivering impassioned speeches urging rebellion against the British. She founded the Irish nationalist version of the Boy Scouts, set up soup kitchens across Dublin to feed the poor and famously advised women to 'dress in suitably short skirts and strong boots, leave your jewels in the bank, and buy a gun'.

During the Easter Rising of 1916, Constance kicked ass. When the Irish rebels were eventually overrun, Constance is famous for having kissed her pistol before surrendering to the Brits with the sassy remark, 'I am ready.' Some iron bars did not stop Constance's rampage for Irish freedom, and shortly after her release she became the first woman to be elected to the British House of Commons. Of course, she refused to take her seat because she was never going to swear an oath of allegiance to the king of England, something all parliamentarians had to do. She went on to be appointed as minister for labour for Sinn Féin and continued her crusade of general badassery.

BADASS RATING: ★★★★★
Whilst imprisoned, Constance organised a ninety-two-woman hunger strike that was so effective she was immediately freed.

CONSTANTIN (also STAN OR TINTIN)

Can you feel creative reverence reverberating up from your pregnant belly? Then name your brilliant baby boy after the dashing and determined Romanian sculptor, Constantin Brâncuşi (1876–1957).

Born in rural Romania, Constantin showed a talent for wood-carving from an early age. His family were peasants and when he was nine years old, Constantin decided that he had had enough of herding sheep and took off to the nearest town. He worked in a grocer's, then as domestic help in a public house before finally making enough money to fund himself through art school.

While Romania was nice, it wasn't exactly the European hotbed of artistic living. So when Paris beckoned, Constantin casually trekked over a thousand miles across Europe on foot, arriving in the French city with nothing more than a small bag on his back and a desperate need for a new pair of shoes.

From eager young sculptor to renowned pioneer of modernism, Constantin created over 250 sculptures in his lifetime. He lived modestly, made all his own furniture out of wood and sported one of the most epic beards in facial hair history.

BADASS RATING: ★ ★ ★
Elusive and mysterious and one of the twentieth century's most influential sculptors.

CRIXUS

Will your future son be super-strong and ready to outwit his overlords? Will he rise up to stand against the establishment? Take inspiration from the Roman gladiator turned freedom fighter and military leader, Crixus (d.72 BC).

Enslaved by the Romans, Crixus was sent away to train as a gladiator. But he was less than pumped at the prospect of spending the next few years wrestling wild animals and other strapping beasts for the sake of entertaining the Roman court, so he rebelled.

Crixus started by forming an army in gladiatorial training school, recruiting over seventy of his fellow prisoners and beefcakes. Together they bust the hell out of there, fought off a small army of Romans sent to recapture them and then set up camp in the mountains. Word got out and more gladiators came to join them until the band of slaves had grown to 150,000 men ready to fight Roman rule. They had a bunch of military victories, including famously abseiling down the cliffs of Mount Garganus behind enemy forces and conquering the Roman camp below.

BADASS RATING: ★ ★ ★ ★
A curly-mopped hulk turned slave warrior and legend.

MORE CRACKING Cs

CALICO

Calico Jack (1682–1720), the Golden Age pirate, hired women onto his crew, designed the iconic Jolly Roger flag and stormed the high seas throughout the eighteenth century.

BADASS RATING: ★★★

CÂNDIDO

Cândido Mariano da Silva Rondon (1865–1958), smart, kind, hardworking and an all-round hardass, Cândido was a Brazilian engineer and Amazon explorer who created a government agency to protect indigenous Indian tribes.

BADASS RATING: ★★★★

CARMEN

Carmen Miranda (1909–55) was a samba singer and Broadway actor, famed for wearing a hat stacked high with fresh fruit – and was the first South American honoured on the Hollywood Walk of Fame.

BADASS RATING: ★★

MORE CRACKING Cs

CAROL

Carol Kaye (b.1935), badass bass guitarist, music legend and powerhouse, has strummed her way through 10,000 recordings, making her the most recorded bassist in history.

BADASS RATING: ★★★★

CARSON

Carson McCullers (1917–67), the uniquely talented, much-admired American author, wrote her first novel, *The Heart is a Lonely Hunter*, when she was just twenty-three.

BADASS RATING: ★★★★

CELIA

Celia Sánchez (1920–80) was a revolutionary powerhouse who played a major role in overthrowing the Cuban dictator, Fulgencio Batista.

BADASS RATING: ★★★★

MORE CRACKING Cs

CLARENCE

Clarence Birdseye (1886–1956) was the scientist who invented the freezer and pioneered frozen food (all HAIL the fish finger, especially when heading into the mouths of little sproglets!).

BADASS RATING: ★★★

CLAUDETTE

Claudette Colvin (b.1939), courageous civil rights activist, refused to give her seat to a white passenger on a bus in Montgomery. This gave Rosa Parks the strength to stand against and demolish segregation.

BADASS RATING: ★★★★

CHRISTABEL

Christabel Pankhurst (1880–1958), a fearless fighter for female emancipation, was an empowering public speaker and suffragette leader.

BADASS RATING: ★★★★

MORE CRACKING Cs

CHRISTINE

Christine de Pizan (1364–c.1430), French author, activist and early feminist, is famous for her revolutionary writing on women and for penning the famous feminist prose, *La Cité des dames*.

BADASS RATING: ★★★★

CILLIAN

Cillian Murphy (b.1976) is a rock singer who ripped up his record contract to become a stage actor, and then went on to kick ass in Hollywood.

BADASS RATING: ★

CLUNY

Cluny Macpherson (1879–1966) was the smart, heroic doctor who invented the gas mask and saved millions of lives.

BADASS RATING: ★★★

MORE CRACKING Cs

CORETTA

Coretta Scott King (1927–2006), American activist, civil rights leader and author known as the First Lady of Civil Rights, dedicated her life to fighting for equality.

BADASS RATING: ★★★★

CORNELIUS

Cornelius Anderson (*c*.1650–*c*.1690) was a bold and tenacious Dutch buccaneer who looted ships, plundered furs and kicked English ass across the coast of Maine.

BADASS RATING: ★

COSTELLO

Elvis Costello (b.1954), rock 'n' roll music legend and avid wearer of giant horn-rimmed glasses, isn't afraid to push musical boundaries or tell the showbiz industry where to go.

BADASS RATING: ★★★

MORE CRACKING Cs

COURTNEY

Courtney Michelle Love (b.1964), husky-voiced musician and shrewd deal-maker, Courtney used Nirvana's recording contract to negotiate herself a million-dollar deal – because why should women earn less than men?

BADASS RATING: ★★★

DAN

Does it feel like your baby bump is performing more somersaults than an entire troupe of jumping, horse-vaulting, horn-blowing clowns? Then heed your abdomen's afflatus and name your child after the charismatic prince of waggery, equestrian jester and star of the circus, Dan Rice (1823–1900).

Applauded as the most accomplished performer in the history of the hippodrome, Dan's clown shows included much singing, dancing, wit and shows of strength. He used a variety of animals in his acts, from a friendly pig to a ballsy rhinoceros; he was known for his burlesque performances of Shakespeare, catching cannon balls on the back of his neck, as well as his booming voice and blow-out gags.

When Dan launched his own circus, he became one of America's highest earners on a salary of a thumping $1,000 a week – not bad for the 1860s. And in later life he swapped his goatee, top hat and striped costume to run for president. As you do.

BADASS RATING: ★★
A first-class performer and king of the carnival.

DARBY

Reckon your little terror will run riot? Perhaps give him the moniker of a lawless, bobby-nobbling, British-Italian gangster, Darby Sabini (1888–1950).

Darby hustled and mobbed his way across Clerkenwell in London, and subsequently Brighton, in the roaring Twenties as the leader of the Sabini gang, also known as the Razors for their cut-throat methods. Darby was ruthless yet charming, and would more than happily deliver a jaw-breaking punch if needed. His gang terrorized the racecourses of southeast England by intimidating bookmakers' rivals and then taking a cut of the cash made on the track. After a few years in the capital, Darby took up residence in Brighton's Grand Hotel, whereupon he sued the local paper for publishing an unattractive character profile on him. A man has gotta keep up his reputation.

BADASS RATING: ★
A ballsy bruiser and Graham Greene's inspiration for the character Colleoni in *Brighton Rock*.

DARWIN

Will your new arrival be curious and clever? Will he go on great adventures and make awe-inspiring discoveries? Then name him after the ground-breaking naturalist, biologist and man they call the godfather of evolutionary science, Charles Darwin (1809–82).

Up until Darwin's life-changing adventure around the world on HMS *Beagle*, he had flirted with careers in taxidermy (pretty badass) and clerical work (less so). So when the golden ticket – in the form of a letter from his Cambridge buddy George Peacock inviting him on board the ship – landed out of the blue on his doormat, Darwin's father was against the voyage. He advised Darwin not to accept, saying something like this: 'Dear son, clearly the crew would have offered the position of naturalist on the expedition to an actual naturalist rather than a clergyman. So I believe the reason he has asked you to join the vessel is because it is doomed and they know something we do not!'

Good job Darwin didn't give a monkey's what his father thought.

BADASS RATING: ★★★★
The brainbox and balls behind the world-changing paper on the theory of evolution.

DASH

Will your squidge have a big imagination? Take inspiration from the fascist-fighting American author and creator of legendary hard-boiled detective characters, Dashiell Hammett (1894–1961).

Dash left school at thirteen and eventually winged his way into a job at the famous Pinkerton's detective agency. But when he was offered a vast fee of $5,000 to ensure that a certain cooper and outspoken unionist met his death, he decided that the world of private investigation was not for him, and he walked out. He turned to his pen and used his previous job as the inspiration for gritty, violent, page-turning stories, introducing the world to badasses like Sam Spade, the fictional private investigator hell-bent on delivering his own form of justice.

BADASS RATING: ★★★
Hailed as the father of the modern detective novel and pioneer of the hard-boiled fiction genre.

DAVID

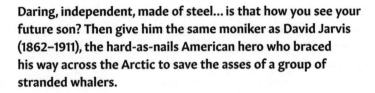

Daring, independent, made of steel... is that how you see your future son? Then give him the same moniker as David Jarvis (1862–1911), the hard-as-nails American hero who braced his way across the Arctic to save the asses of a group of stranded whalers.

In the winter of 1897, tragedy struck at Point Barrow in Alaska when 265 men were marooned on the ice, trapped in sub-zero temperatures with diminishing food supplies. Enter David, the fearless saviour who herded together 400 reindeers and then smashed his way across hazardous lands, enduring the most extreme weather and temperatures of –45 degrees on the rescue mission of a lifetime. He fought off polar bears, frostbite and blinding snowstorms, all while navigating the treacherous terrain of 3,000-foot drops and icy inclines to save the entire fleet of sailors.

BADASS RATING: ★★★★
Risked both his testicles and more to save hundreds of lives.

DAVY

Will your son be at home surrounded by trees and wild creatures? Will he enjoy travelling across uninhabited lands? Then consider the namesake Davy Crockett (1786–1836), the legendary American adventurer and politician.

Walt Disney claimed that Davy killed a bear with his own hands when he was just three, but whether or not this is 100 per cent true, no one can deny that he was one tough nut.

When a school bully had a go at him, Davy floored him. But so brutal was his self-defence, Davy decided he'd be better off fleeing to the woods to stick it out on his own than facing the consequences. He spent the next few years travelling across Tennessee and making ends meet hunting wild beasts and generally living rough in the wilderness. One winter Davy went on an almighty bear-slaying spree, claiming to have slain 105 of the brown furry grizzlies in just seven months.

BADASS RATING: ★★
Woodsman and alleged king of the wild frontier.

DELIA

Is the spirit of adventure calling you through your new baby girl? Better name her after an explorer, then. So how about early anthropologist Delia Akeley (1875–1970)?

A conservationist and a skilled hunter, Delia travelled extensively across Africa with her husband, taxidermist Carl Akeley. She is famous for taking down and preserving a big bull elephant now displayed in the American Museum of Natural History. During her adventures she also discovered new species of birds and antelopes, collected artefacts and spent a season living among the Bambuti pygmies of the Ituri Forest in Congo.

One night, during her travels through Boma, Delia came face to face with a lion. She quickly fired a bullet in self-defence, but it only grazed his backbone: he was wounded badly enough to fall, but was still alive and ready to seek revenge. Unable to escape, Delia hid behind some branches, where she stayed all night. Every time the lion roared, she could feel his breath on her face. When dawn broke and she could see more than just his outline at the end of her nose, she shot him and ran to safety.

From scrambling up trees in Uganda to flee a herd of elephants to travelling across dangerous mountains in Kenya to save her husband after an animal attack, Delia was courageous and strong – and principled, too. She once adopted a monkey, brought him back to New York and named him J. T. Junior. He may have bitten her leg and smelled so bad that guests stopping coming over, but Delia loved him so fiercely that when her husband suggested she put him in a zoo, she promptly filed for divorce.

BADASS RATING: ★★★
A hot-tempered adventurer with no fear.

DESMOND

Will your little champ be loyal, faithful and dedicated? You could consider naming him after the war hero who refused to kill, Desmond Doss (1919–2006).

A devout Christian and a pacifist, Desmond volunteered to kick fascist ass in the Second World War – just without the use of any form of violence. He vowed that he would never take the life of another and refused to carry any weapons in combat. Who needs guns when you have monumentally gigantic balls like Desmond's, anyway?

His initial assignment was serving as a medic in Okinawa, Japan, and the first day of battle was ferocious. American soldiers were pinned down by gunfire and hundreds of lives were lost, but in walked Desmond – a truly fearless warrior who was badass enough to take on the enemy with nothing more than a piece of rope and an unbelievable amount of ballsery. Desmond crawled through the night, ducking the crossfire in torrential rain, and relentlessly risked his life to drag his comrades to safety. In one evening, the man singlehandedly saved the lives of seventy-five soldiers. What a man!

BADASS RATING: ★★★★★
The first conscientious objector ever to earn the Medal of Honor – America's highest award for military bravery.

DIANE

So your little sweetie-pie is going to know what she wants, and then go out and own it? Sounds like you should name her after the formidable designer, philanthropist and one-time princess, Diane von Fürstenberg (b.1946).

As a teenager, Diane faked appendicitis, insisting a surgeon remove her appendix purely so that she could dodge some tiresome exams and instead enjoy the summer catching rays in the garden, and most likely plotting how to launch a fashion empire. Her first attempt at doing so left her bankrupt, but a woman like Diane doesn't give up easily.

She went on to invent the wrap dress (she sold five million of them in one year alone), launch one of the most successful fashion brands in history and establish herself as a global icon.

BADASS RATING: ★★★
A risk-taking tour de force of the fashion industry and a badass, independent woman.

Dietrich

Kind, caring, fearsome: if these three attributes are the sort you'd like your son to aim for, how about linking him to German pastor, spy and anti-Nazi rebel, Dietrich Bonhoeffer (1906–45)?

A man of God and intense moral courage, Dietrich turned into a political conspirator and anti-Nazi double agent during the Second World War. He smuggled Jews into Switzerland, performed illegal sermons throughout Germany and risked his life on numerous occasions in order to help kick Gestapo ass. He is most famous for assisting the assassination attempt on Adolf Hitler, codenamed Operation Valkyrie.

BADASS RATING: ★★★★
The fearless theologian who formed a resistance against the Führer.

DOLLY

Are you growing a girl who will stay true to herself? Will she follow her dreams and achieve greatness? Then join her in spirit to the flamboyant, big-haired, big-hearted queen of country music, Dolly Parton (b.1946).

Oozing with confidence and sass, Dolly came from a dirt-poor family and went on to become one of the most successful singers in history. A woman of exceptional talent, she can bust out tunes on nine different instruments from the piano to the banjo to the harp. She has written over 3,000 songs, sold over 10 million albums, owns a large number of Grammys plus her own theme park, Dollyworld, and a charity that gives free books to schools. She even once told Elvis to back the F off when he asked to record one of her songs.

BADASS RATING: ★★★★
An insanely talented woman who has always stood up for herself and worked it like a boss.

Dora

Are you convinced your future daughter will grow up to be artistic, intelligent, kind-hearted but with a fiery side? Then name her after the fascist-fighting surrealist painter, photographer, poet and muse, Dora Maar (1907–97).

French-born Dora grew up in Buenos Aires before returning to Paris to study photography at the Académie Julian, a school she selected for its equal teachings to both men and women. Dora mixed in intellectual circles, set up various studios across Paris and became widely known as the rising star in surrealist circles. She wasn't afraid to take to the streets to capture the effects of the Depression, and often participated in anti-fascist demonstrations.

Dora wooed Pablo Picasso in 1935 when she strutted into the Café Les Deux Magots wearing jet-black gloves embroidered with roses. She sat down opposite him and proceeded to stab a small penknife between each of her fingers and onto the table, missing every so often so that drops of blood fell from the roses embroidered on her gloves. Picasso, attracted to her danger (and blatant disrespect for café tables), immediately went over to introduce himself. They fast became lovers and Picasso regularly painted portraits of Dora, including the well-known *Weeping Woman* and *Dora Maar Seated*.

Dora once famously wrestled Picasso's ex-lover Marie-Thérèse Walter in the street, and whilst her affair with Picasso did not last, she has a place in history as the ultimate artist's iconoclast.

BADASS RATING: ★★★
Sassy, strong-minded and smart.

DOT/DOTTIE

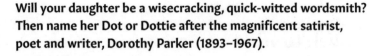

**Will your daughter be a wisecracking, quick-witted wordsmith?
Then name her Dot or Dottie after the magnificent satirist,
poet and writer, Dorothy Parker (1893–1967).**

A woman who would throw open the front door to greet her guests
with the quip, 'What fresh hell can this be?', Dot was the master of
the one-liner. In her twenties, she lived in New York and wrote for
Vogue and *Vanity Fair*, but the latter gave her the boot for her sharp
tongue and for lampooning too many producers – even though
readers adored her reviews. Dot invented *The New Yorker* short story;
she was dark, authentic; her poetry collection received glowing
critiques, and her screenwriting was nominated for two Oscars. Dot
married and divorced; she had lovers in abundance, but for all the
passion, there was heartache. When terminating a pregnancy with a
devastatingly unreliable lover, she later consoled, 'I put all my eggs in
one bastard!'

A late starter to activism, Dot gave the fist to fascism by declaring
herself a communist. Did she care when she was blacklisted from
Hollywood for her political stance? Did she fuck. Dot eventually left
her estate to Martin Luther King: from one badass to another.

BADASS RATING: ★★★★
Queen of banter and biting, satirical wit, Dorothy Parker is the
definition of sass. Her epitaph reads: 'Excuse my dust'.

MORE DAUNTLESS Ds

DANUTA

Danuta Danielsson (1947–88) was a ball-busting avenger who smacked a marching neo-Nazi with her handbag – right across his fascist little head. The moment was caught on camera and plastered across the press; but, like a true badass, Danuta refused to share her story.

BADASS RATING: ★★★★

DEDE

Dede Mirabal (1925–2014) was an activist and revolutionary who, along with her no-nonsense-taking sisters, helped topple the cruel Dominican Republic dictator Rafael Trujillo.

BADASS RATING: ★★★★

DINO

Dino De Laurentiis (1919–2010), the risk-taking, bangin' Italian-born film producer, had over 500 films to his name.

BADASS RATING: ★

MORE DAUNTLESS Ds

DIXIE

Dixie Bibb Graves (1882–1965), from Alabama, was an activist, feminist, philanthropist and the first female senator.

BADASS RATING: ★

DODIE

Dodie Bellamy (unknown–), the unapologetic, experimental feminist writer and poet, and true boundary-busting badass.

BADASS RATING: ★ ★ ★

DON

A banging batsman, Australian-born **Don Bradman** (1908–2001) is the greatest cricketer of all time with an exceptional performance record – still unbeaten today.

BADASS RATING: ★ ★ ★

MORE DAUNTLESS Ds

DONNA

Donna Tartt (b.1963) is a cool AF, devastatingly sharp writer, who gifted the world with her literary sensation *The Secret History*.

BADASS RATING: ★★★★

DORIS

Doris Lessing (1919–2013), an insightful, witheringly smart writer and feminist and prolific ground-breaking, genre-busting novelist, was the eleventh woman to be awarded the Nobel Prize for Literature.

BADASS RATING: ★★★★

DOUGLAS

Douglas Bader (1910–82) was the British fighter pilot who, after losing both legs, whipped more Nazi ass in air combat during the Second World War than anyone else on the British squad.

BADASS RATING: ★★★

MORE DAUNTLESS Ds

DYLAN

Dylan Marlais Thomas (1914–53), a controversial genius, hailed as the greatest British poet of all time and a man who could drink eighteen whiskies straight. Badass!

BADASS RATING: ★★★★

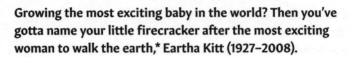

EARTHA

Growing the most exciting baby in the world? Then you've gotta name your little firecracker after the most exciting woman to walk the earth,* Eartha Kitt (1927–2008).

Singer, actor, civil rights advocate and political provocateur, Eartha was known for her purring sultry tones, beauty and refusal to compromise her beliefs, even when it led to her being blacklisted by the CIA.

Born on the cotton fields in South Carolina, Eartha was the illegitimate child of a plantation owner's son and a Cherokee woman, which didn't make for the easiest start in life. At the age of sixteen, a chance bet with a friend led her to win a scholarship with the esteemed Katherine Dunham Dance Company, and despite being told her bust was too big for Broadway, Eartha danced in *Blue Holiday* in New York. She went on to perform across the world in theatres, on film and television as well as building a legendary career as a solo artist. One of the first mixed race women to land a leading role in Hollywood, Eartha broke boundaries in her role of Catwoman in *Batman*; somehow she managed to turn a portly man with a white beard into a sex symbol in her festive jingle, 'Santa Baby'; she had a string of Number 1 chart bestsellers; and she fearlessly stood up in the White House to oppose the Vietnam War, despite it costing her her career for a while.

* According to Orson Welles, *c.*1950.

BADASS RATING: ★★★
A cultural icon who dared to step outside the lines.

EDDIE

Will your little rug-rat be bright, easily bored and have a taste for disobedience? Take inspiration from the petty criminal turned British double agent, Eddie Chapman (1914–77).

After a turbulent childhood, Eddie joined the army, but quickly became tired of military life and absconded after he met a girl on a night on the razz in Soho. A man who enjoyed a lavish lifestyle of booze, betting and bonking, he was led to a career of crime in order to keep up with his financiers. Known for relentlessly dodging the nick, he once threw himself head-first out of a closed dining room window to swerve the cops. But they eventually caught up with him and sent him to jail in Jersey, where, in an extraordinary turn of events, his career as a spy began.

Eddie was recruited by the Germans during their invasion of the Channel Islands. Once trained in the art of espionage, he was then flown back to England to sabotage an airfield. He accidentally parachuted into Norfolk after getting his bottom stuck in the hatch of the plane, and this led him to switch loyalties to MI5, adopt the name of Agent ZigZag and become one of the most iconic double agents of the Second World War.

BADASS RATING: ★★★★
The badass who went from blowing up safes to blowing up Nazis. His final career move? Running a spa in Hertfordshire. No jokes.

EDITH

Is your baby kicking so hard you think she might judo-flip her way out into the world? Why not name her after the small but mighty suffragette and martial arts supremo, Edith Margaret Garrud (1872–1971)?

Edith trained in the art of jiu-jitsu, a martial art specializing in the use of brains over brutality by taking down opponents with a gentle nudge to a sensitive pressure point. During the early twentieth century, she set up a training school to teach other women how to fight like queens, building a thirty-strong team of her best jiu-jitsu students and fellow suffragettes. These women were known as The Bodyguard and were on hand at any given moment to perform dangerous duties, which basically meant protecting other suffragettes by beating the shit out of the cops usually twice their height and weight. The band of sisters hid clubs in their dresses or under hoop skirts and barbed wire in bouquets, and slayed police with style during the increasingly feverish campaign to give women the right to vote. BADASS.

BADASS RATING: ★★★★★
The high-kicking ninja who showed the world how to fight.

EDMUND

Will your future son dare to achieve the impossible? Will he possess strength, bravery and endurance? Then name him after the record-breaking New Zealand athlete and mountaineer who never stopped pushing his abilities to the limit, Sir Edmund Hillary (1919–2008).

Before 1953, no one had ever made it to the top of Mount Everest, although there had been many attempts. When John Hunt led the ninth British expedition to the mountain, a few people were surprised to find Edmund – a shy, studious and lanky Kiwi – on the team.

After a gruelling journey across the Khumbu Icefall, the first duo were assigned by the expedition's leader to climb to the summit, but due to exhaustion they turned back. Edmund and guide Tenzing Norgay were the back-up pair, so when the others returned, off they trotted to attempt the impossible. They ascended steep ice-covered slopes, fought altitude sickness and ripping winds, grappled with oxygen masks and ploughed across treacherous terrain. On 29 May 1953, first Edmund then Tenzing climbed almost 30,000 feet into the sky and stood at the peak of Mount Everest – making history.

BADASS RATING: ★ ★ ★ ★ ★
The first man to conquer the unconquerable by climbing to the peak of Mount Everest and returning ALIVE.

EDNA

Does playing scrabble feature big in your family? Maybe the next to arrive will be a master wordsmith? Take inspiration from the outspoken, outrageously talented and much-loved American poet, Edna St Vincent Millay (1882–1950).

Edna wrote her first critically acclaimed poem, *Renascence*, at just twenty years old and became the third woman to ever win the Pulitzer Prize in 1923 for *The Ballad of the Harp Weaver*. She coined the excellent phrase 'to burn the candle at both ends' and, being openly bisexual, she had a lot of male and female lovers – which she delighted in causing much shock among the American bourgeoisie.

An unreserved activist and feminist, Edna spoke out against sexism and class; her writing often had strong political undertones. When she married, she shunned the conventions of her time and her husband gave up his career to help her manage her own. Damn straight.

BADASS RATING: ★★★★
An iconoclast of feminism, rebellion and literary freedom and ultimate word slinger.

Edward

So you're going to give birth to a force of nature: your kid will be determined, tough and fearsome. Right? Well, how about naming him after the towering, toothless, devil-toasting freebooter, Edward Teach, aka Blackbeard (1680–1718).

Known for deliberately engulfing his entire head of hair in flames before charging into battle, Edward had the longest, blackest, smokiest beard in pirate history. Armed with a minimum of three pistols, a knife for every day of the week and a cutlass bigger than many of the men it slaughtered, Edward was the most gruesome pirate in existence.

But one day, he decided it was time to hang up his tricorn and stop terrorizing the seas, so he marooned his entire crew on a faraway island, stole all their plunder and abandoned them there. With all the extra booty, he bought himself a spiffing retirement home in the sun and even managed to get a job as a privateer.

But Edward couldn't resist the force of the pirate within him. Soon he was looting and hornswaggling his way through choppy waters once again, bellowing, 'Once a pirate, always a pirate, me hearty! Arrghhhhhh!' before sinking his teeth into treasure.

BADASS RATING: ★★★★
The most feared pirate to ride a wave of terror across the Caribbean.

EFFIE

Do you hope to inspire your daughter to live out her ambitions, no matter how big they are? You could set her on her way – make her the namesake of a magnificent motorbike-riding ball of fire, Effie Hotchkiss (b. *c.*1889).

Bored with her job as a bank clerk in New York City, Effie pined for adventure and longed to feel the wind whip through her hair. So in 1915, she purchased a Harley-Davidson V-twin, donned leather riding breeches and set off on the American road trip of a lifetime – with her mother Avis tucked into the sidecar.

From Brooklyn to San Francisco and back again, the duo went pedal to the metal, storming across treacherous terrain, down mud tracks and pothole-covered roads. They braced sub-zero temperatures, kept cool in sweltering heat of over 120 degrees and shrugged off floods like spray showers. They improvised with blankets when they ran out of inner tubes, fought off wild animals and powered through hunger when supplies got low. Completing the 9,000-mile trip in just a few months, Effie and her equally badass mum become the twentieth century's first transcontinental female motorcyclists. Legends.

BADASS RATING: ★★★★
A daring and dauntless petrolhead.

EILEEN

What parent wouldn't want their girl to reach for the stars and follow her dreams? Perhaps she could even follow in the footsteps of the determined, boundary-busting astronaut, Eileen Collins (b.1956).

Eileen trained as a pilot, then joined NASA as an astronaut. In 1995 she became the first female to pilot a mission in space, and went on to become the first woman to command a space shuttle mission in 1999. Over her career, she clocked up over 872 space flying hours and became the first ever astronaut to guide a space shuttle through a 360-degree pitch manoeuvre, which basically meant she flipped her rocket nose to tail. When asked if she ever felt scared during spaceflight, she nonchalantly shrugged, 'I don't think I really had any fear of danger... if it's going to be something that you have no control over, then why worry about it?' Badass.

BADASS RATING: ★★★★★
A fearless adventurer who has made a giant leap for womankind.

EINSTEIN/EINIE

If you're convinced your boy's going to be fiercely smart and a total rebel, you could take inspiration from one of the biggest badasses in history, Albert Einstein (1879–1955).

Not one for bowing down to military-style dictation, Einstein gave school the boot after a series of major bust-ups with his teachers. Rather than kick back on the couch playing *World of Warcraft* like a normal teenager, he left school to instead spend his time devouring three-volume scientific textbooks, eventually gaining a place at a college in Switzerland where he continued his casual disrespect for any form of authority.

From sexual mores to politics and physics, Einstein was an impertinent nonconformist. He gave zero f**ks about his appearance, shunning socks, hairdressers and any form of smart attire in favour of bare feet, tracksuit bottoms, loose shirts and a wild, free mane of hair. He smoked like a trooper, shirked the whole marriage before kids thing, shagged whomever he liked and eventually ran off with his cousin. He defied political labels and campaigned for racial equality and civil rights. He thought little of the mainstream physics of his time, invented the theory of relativity, won a Nobel Prize and became the biggest name synonymous with brainbox in history.

He also casually turned down the chance to become president of Israel because he was seventy-four by that point, and frankly wanted a rest.

BADASS RATING: ★★★★★
A contrary free thinker, iconoclast, physics punk and completely extraordinary human.

Eleanor

Will your little nipper be a trailblazing, smart-as-hell crusader who will work tirelessly to create an equal world? Then name her after the social reform campaigner, suffragette, Westminster politician and woman who pioneered the child benefit system, Eleanor Florence Rathbone (1872–1946).

An Oxford graduate, Eleanor was reserved and determined. She dedicated her life to making the world a better place – from campaigning for cheaper milk and benefits for children and the unemployed, to getting money to war widows or fighting against slum housing.

She went from local politics in Liverpool to Westminster, where she stood her ground in a male-dominated arena. Her maiden speech exposed and opposed female genital mutilation in the British colony of Kenya. She fiercely believed that mothers should be paid for the work of raising children (damn right) and pushed a proposal for the introduction of Family Allowance to give mothers independence. Just before her death, the Family Allowance Act was passed into law, creating a legacy that has empowered infinite women and their families.

BADASS RATING: ★★★★
A woman who demanded society's acknowledgement that raising the future is a job, and should be valued as such.

ELFREDA/ELFIE

Gusty, gifted and galvanic: if you think these words are going to match your new arrival, how about naming her after the courageous activist, Elfreda Reyes (1901–92)?

When Elfie worked at the home of a white British family in Belize, she demanded a minimum wage of $5 a week. She got the wage she asked for, then set out to ensure that other domestic workers in Belize did so, too – by launching a national campaign for a minimum wage for labourers. A social reform warrior, Elfie co-founded the Jobless Workers' Union and pushed to change the laws over wages and hours. She set up a day care centre to help working mothers and fought for the economic and political freedom of women.

An empowering public speaker, Elfie was a voice against the British Empire, and it is partly thanks to her activism that men and women in Belize were both simultaneously granted the right to vote in 1953.

BADASS RATING: ★★★★
A brave and inspiring warrior.

ELIJAH

Will your babe be born inquisitive, with problem-solving superpowers? Will he build Lego masterpieces? Then name him after the ingenious African-American inventor, Elijah McCoy (1843–1929).

Born in Canada to runaway slaves, Elijah was so brainy at school he was awarded a scholarship to study engineering at Edinburgh University. But on graduation he was forced into a job shovelling fuel into boilers because his contemporaries didn't think a black man was capable of being an engineer. So he proved them wrong and singlehandedly invented a whole load of really useful shit, including a world-changing solution to one of the biggest challenges then facing steam engine travel.

His creations were so outstanding that over time his surname became a catchphrase for damn good quality – Elijah is the 'real McCoy'.

BADASS RATING: ★★★
Elijah patented over fifty items, making him one of the greatest inventors of the nineteenth century.

ELIOT

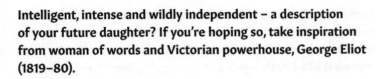

Intelligent, intense and wildly independent – a description of your future daughter? If you're hoping so, take inspiration from woman of words and Victorian powerhouse, George Eliot (1819–80).

With an insatiable appetite for stories, Eliot was well read but often felt irked by her fellow lady writers for delivering what she deemed shallow and simplistic plots. She basically wanted more female characters that were badass. So she created them. Women that didn't run off into the sunset, or live happily ever after, but were instead tortured by their environments and sometimes led to do terrible things.

From nailing it as the literary editor at the leftist publication *The Westminster Review* to becoming the richest woman in the country through selling a shitload of novels, Eliot smashed through gender barriers as a truly independent woman.

BADASS RATING: ★★★
A visionary, chick-lit-smashing powerhouse and legendary author.

ELIZABETH

Could you do with a doctor in the family? Or maybe you just hope your little nipper will be caring, compassionate and determined to follow her own path? Either way, you could name her after the whip-smart, pioneering female physician, Elizabeth Garrett Anderson (1836–1917).

Determined to become a doctor, Elizabeth applied to various medical schools across the UK but got rejected on the grounds of her gender. So instead, she enrolled onto the nursing programme at Middlesex Hospital, then snuck into the lectures for trainee doctors. There was outcry at her presence, but Elizabeth batted off the bigots with grace. After years of sneaking in to study medicine, she then demanded that she be allowed to sit the exams to qualify as a physician, given that the Society of Apothecaries didn't specifically forbid women from doing so. She smashed the exams and qualified as a doctor in 1865.

BADASS RATING: ★★★★★
The first British woman doctor and surgeon.

ELIZE OR BETH? (ELIZEBETH)

Will your baby be energetic, impatient, a born problem-solver and smart AF? Then it sounds like she'll have plenty in common with the code-busting, secret-smashing cryptanalyst and poet, Elizebeth Friedman (1892–1980).

Elizebeth taught herself to break codes while working for Riverbank Laboratories in her early twenties. She had left employment as a school principal because she had found playing referee to a playground of kids a little yawnsome and upon looking for career change, she had stumbled across this private research facility. Initially she was taken on to help a team of scholars try to prove that Sir Francis Bacon was, in fact, the author of Shakespeare's plays. Once all the great man's sonnets had been rather unsuccessfully combed through for evidence of Bacon's tongue, Elizebeth, alongside her future husband William Friedman, decided it was time to start a new project and together went on to develop ridiculously smart methods that would underpin modern cryptology.

Elizebeth unscrambled secret codes in order to smash up spy rings and outsmart gangsters. She painstakingly interpreted and decoded radio messages to stop international drug and alcohol smugglers dead in their tracks; she busted a million-dollar bootleg rum operation and thwarted a ring of Chinese opium smugglers.

When the Second World War broke out, Elizebeth intercepted thousands of Nazi wireless messages sent from South America to Germany, which some might argue singlehandedly saved the Americas from Nazi rule.

BADASS RATING: ★★★★
A lot of bad stuff didn't happen thanks to Elizebeth's genius mind, and her code-cracking mad skills.

ELLEN

Will your little bird be earnest and inspiring, and excel in science and maths? If so, consider making her the namesake of the chemist, sanitation engineer and visionary who pioneered better water and air quality across America, Ellen Swallow Richards (1842–1911).

In 1896, Ellen surveyed the water supply of the population of Massachusetts and discovered that thousands of children were falling seriously ill because of the illegal conditions in schools: buildings lacked ventilation or proper fire escapes, arsenic was in the wallpaper, there were open sewer pipes, floors that had never been washed and filthy toilets. Children were dying, but these 'murders', as Ellen called them, were entirely preventable. Ellen's work laid the foundations for the establishment of water quality standards and modern sewage treatment plants, which in turn has saved countless lives across America.

BADASS RATING: ★★★★
A remarkable scientist who fought for change. And won.

ELSA

Want to inspire your little bean to use her imagination to create the extraordinary? Then name her after the rebel fashion designer and queen of the outrageous, Elsa Schiaparelli (1890–1973).

After graduating from university, Elsa wrote and published a saucy poetry book, which went down like a lead balloon with her high-minded family of Italian nobility. Disgraced, Elsa was shunted off to a convent. But being the badass boss that she was, Elsa went on hunger strike before busting out of the abbey and fleeing to England.

Between London and New York, she married, birthed, divorced and found herself a single mum struggling to make ends meet. After becoming friends with a group of artists selling boutique French fashions, she moved to Paris and started to make clothes. Whatever she lacked in formal training, Elsa made up with courage. She introduced the world to shocking pink, animal prints, brooch-like buttons and shoulder pads. Elsa transformed fashion. She invented the culotte – neither trouser, nor skirt – just bottom wear living life by its own rules. She created lobster dresses, shoe hats and rebellious gloves with red fingernails painted on. She was an extraordinary designer who dared to create bold and outrageous designs. And lest we forget, this bona fide badass gave the world leopard print. Amen.

BADASS RATING: ★★★★
The violet of vogue and master of reinvention who turned clothing into an art form.

EMELINE

Are you growing a little rebel? The world has spawned a few, but none quite like the fearless, daring American Civil War spy and smuggler, Emeline Pigott (1836–1919).

Born in North Carolina, Emeline was twenty-five when the Civil War broke out. With a love of danger and rebellion in equal measure, she sashayed up to the Confederate army and offered her services. First she worked as a nurse, then collected and distributed mail, food and clothing supplies, leaving stashes for Confederate soldiers in marked hollow trees. Later she became a fully fledged spy with a total disregard for her own life. She threw lavish parties for Union soldiers, where she would lure them into the soft crease of her bosom and encourage them to get hammered on cheap wine so she could extract classified information to pass on to the other side. She wore voluminous dresses with giant pockets stuffed full of important papers and documents, the most confidential information sewn into the hoop of her skirt. She'd then travel across North Carolina, risking her life, to hand out secret intelligence to the Confederate army.

BADASS RATING: ★★★
When the Unionists captured her, Emeline ate the contents of her skirt and escaped the death penalty. Badass.

EMMA

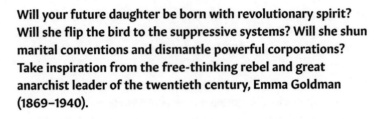

Will your future daughter be born with revolutionary spirit? Will she flip the bird to the suppressive systems? Will she shun marital conventions and dismantle powerful corporations? Take inspiration from the free-thinking rebel and great anarchist leader of the twentieth century, Emma Goldman (1869–1940).

Emma's critics called her the 'most dangerous woman in America', clearly because they feared she might succeed in her mission to give a voice to the oppressed. Emma's philosophy was that everyone should have personal freedom and the right to self-expression, and she was going to make damn sure she was heard.

Born in Lithuania, Emma fled to America to escape an arranged marriage, defying her Jewish parents. She was furious that society expected her to simply produce children and put dinner on the table. A fiery public speaker, she toured the world championing sexual freedom, gay rights and workers' rights, to name a few. She disseminated birth control literature and told the unemployed to take bread from the rich. Trailed, harassed and persecuted by police for her campaigning, Emma faced imprisonment, violence and deportation. But despite best efforts to stop her, Emma continued her voyage and became one of the most inspiring, radical and badass thinkers of the twentieth century.

Badass quote: 'Women need not always keep their mouths shut and their wombs open.'

BADASS RATING: ★★★★★
Anarchist facilitator and organizer and totally badass.

EMMELINE

Some names are simply synonymous with rebellion and revolution. If it's one of those you're after, look no further than the leader of the British women's suffrage movement, Emmeline Pankhurst (1858–1928).

Emmeline spent her life fighting for women's freedom. She was the founder of the Women's Social and Political Union, a woman-only group dedicated to getting voting rights for women, which she set up in 1903 with the slogan 'Deeds not Words'. Emmeline encouraged confrontation and militant tactics to project the voice of suffrage. She smashed windows, hurled rocks through the glass of 10 Downing Street, burnt shit to the ground and defaced artwork as part of the fight to give women a voice. She even egged on her pal Mary to walk into the National Gallery wielding a meat cleaver, which she then full on swung into the naked derrière of Diego Velázquez's *Rokeby Venus*. Take that patriarchy!

In and out of prison like a yoyo as a result of her campaigning, it was Emmeline who masterminded the suffragette hunger strikes. Spirited, courageous and persistent, she eventually led her sisters to victory, partially in 1918 and then completely in 1928. Total badass.

BADASS RATING: ★ ★ ★ ★ ★
The powerhouse who brought down the patriarchy and won the right for women to vote.

EMMY

Could you be carrying a little wonder? A prodigy? It does happen. If you are, you could inspire her to unleash her genius on the world by naming her after the mathematics revolutionary, Emmy Noether (1882–1935).

Emmy was so hot for numbers that she snuck into the back of university lecture halls to informally give herself a formal education. Women were banned from universities in Germany at the time, but that didn't stop Emmy wangling an honorary degree. How? She had the balls to sit the 'forbidden' exams and when she passed them with mind-blowing brilliance, the officials were compelled to break convention and award her with a certificate. Damn straight.

Emmy was recruited by Albert Einstein to work at the University of Göttingen, where he was developing the theory of relativity, and there she worked for seven years on zero pay before being finally allowed to take home a token salary. During her time, she made ground-breaking contributions to the fields of abstract algebra and physics, developing her own theorem which has since been hailed as the backbone of modern physics.

When Emmy was fired from her post for her Jewish heritage, she continued to teach in secret. Whilst some historians may have 'accidentally' overlooked her, many would argue that Emmy was one of the greatest scientific brains of all time.

BADASS RATING: ★★★★
So damn smart that even Einstein was intimidated.

Erasmus

Want your son to grow up a free thinker? Will he be generous, energetic and a little bit cheeky? As an Erasmus, he could take after the British doctor, poet and maverick, Erasmus Darwin (1731–1802).

Most well known as Charles Darwin's grandfather, Erasmus was probably the most badass of all the Darwins. He had ideas and ideals way ahead of his time. As a physicist, he believed strongly that the mind and body were entirely interlinked. He was pro-equality and sought social reform. He fought hard to teach society about the abuses of the slave trade, championed education for women and founded one of the first schools in the Midlands, which his daughters then ran.

He also wrote beautiful poetry, was an avid inventor and came up with the idea that all life came from one common ancestor.

BADASS RATING: ★ ★ ★ ★
Unafraid to voice radical ideas, Erasmus earned a place in history as one of the most original thinkers of the eighteenth century.

ERIC

Will your son enjoy playing pranks? Will you teach him to 'fake it until you make it'? Then you might want to name him after the badass of the art world – bold and brazen art forger, Eric Hebborn (1934–96).

Eric was expelled from school at the age of eight for burning it down. He was then moved down to Essex where he channelled his energy into art school instead, prioritizing painting over pyromania, much to the relief of his teachers.

His work never quite received critical acclaim, so to prove that the art world knew jack shit, he started mimicking the likes of Michelangelo, Rembrandt and Claude. Eric duped dealers into selling his work on as originals for many years, and to this day no one is quite sure how many of his forgeries are sitting masquerading as the works of other long-dead painters in museums and galleries across the world.

BADASS RATING: ★★★★
The most infamous art fraudster of modern times.

ERNEST

Do you hope your son will chase fun and adventure (and also really like cats)? If so, you could make him the namesake of the certified badass, feline-loving literary rebel and legend, Ernest Miller Hemingway (1899–1961).

A Nobel Prize-winning writer and one of history's great artists, Ernest also happened to lead an extreme life of badassery. Here are some examples:

1. At the age of three he shot and killed a porcupine. And then ate it.*
2. It is believed he may have led a dangerous double life as a secret spy for both Soviet and US intelligence.
3. He was a man with an uncanny ability to escape death. Ernest survived two plane crashes (within a two-day period), a ruptured kidney, a ruptured spleen, a ruptured liver, a crushed vertebra, a fractured skull, mortar shrapnel wounds, three car crashes and bushfire burns. Only a true badass would choose exactly when and how to go...
4. He once stole a urinal from his favourite watering hole, declaring, 'I pissed away so much of my money in that urinal that I own it.'

*We do not condone this behaviour.

BADASS RATING: ★★★★★
A great American novelist who spent his life in the pursuit of adventure.

ERNESTINE

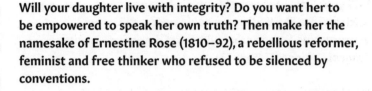

Will your daughter live with integrity? Do you want her to be empowered to speak her own truth? Then make her the namesake of Ernestine Rose (1810–92), a rebellious reformer, feminist and free thinker who refused to be silenced by conventions.

Ernestine was born in Poland into a Jewish family. From a young age she felt enraged that women were treated as inferior to men. By the time she was a teenager, she had outright rejected her religion on the basis of its oppressive attitudes.

When her mother died, her father made the foolish mistake of thinking he could simply marry off Ernestine to one of his younger friends, in the knowledge that if she broke the contract she would have to forgo her inheritance. But Ernestine was having absolutely none of this bullshit. She spurned the marriage, sued her father for her share of the estate – and won. Don't mess with Ernestine.

A free woman with enough bang to travel the world, Ernestine headed towards Berlin and then London where, along with Robert Owen, she went about campaigning for the rights of all people, no matter what sex, race or class. From London to New York, she spoke out for social reform and equality, making sure her voice – as well as everyone else's – was heard.

BADASS RATING: ★★★★
An outspoken atheist, hailed as 'queen of the platform' for her eloquent and empowering speeches.

EUGÈNE

**Will your little life barnacle crave excitement and intrigue?
With a name like Eugène, he could become like the
venturesome French criminal turned detective, Eugène
François Vidocq (1775–1857).**

It all began when teenage Eugène accidentally killed his fencing
instructor. In a panic he fled his hometown and spent several months
on the run before joining the French army. He made a name for
himself on the battlefield before overstepping the mark with one of
his officers. Rather than face the consequences, which would have
most likely involved a noose around his neck, Eugène went on the
run again.

Enjoying an illustrious life of petty crime, pub brawls, forgeries and
a brief stint as a pirate, Eugene spent the next decade consistently
going to jail and then busting himself out with a variety of canny
tricks – from simple things like forging parole papers or disguising
himself as a sailor to throwing himself out of a prison window. He
was so good at foiling the authorities that one day Eugène decided it
might be better for everyone if he instead offered his services to the
police and worked as a spy. And so he did, becoming one of the best
private detectives in France.

BADASS RATING: ★★★
**A legendary crook turned crime-solver whose life may have
inspired the character Sherlock Holmes.**

EVA

Are you growing a tiny human who is caring, compassionate and capricious? Why not name her after the woman who captivated Argentina and then the world, Eva Perón (1919–52)?

Eva grew up in rural poverty before making her way to Buenos Aires to work as an actor. After meeting Juan Perón at a charity event, Eva married him and together they campaigned for his presidency, something that raised an eyebrow or two at the time; it was certainly unconventional. As first lady, Eva devoted herself to helping those in need as well as fighting for female equality. She founded a political party for women, advocated workers' rights, improved Argentina's healthcare system and built orphanages and hospitals in abundance.

While battling aggressive cancer, she ran for office as vice president – what a total powerhouse – but eventually had to pull out of the campaign. She died shortly after her thirty-third birthday. She was an icon, a legend and a badass who dared to make a better world.

BADASS RATING: ★★★★
Called a sinner, called a saint and immortalized in a musical by Andrew Lloyd Webber.

MORE ELECTRIC Es

Eben

Eben Etzebeth (b.1991) is a hard-as-nails, world-class rugby player who can bench press 175 kilos (385 lbs).

BADASS RATING: ★

Edson

Edson Arantes do Nascimento (also known as Pelé) (b.1940) is basically the greatest footballer that has ever lived and an all-round rad human being.

BADASS RATING: ★★★★★

Elam

Helen Elam Van Winkle, aka Baddie Winkle (b.1928), is the sensational nonagenarian instagran who has been giving zero fucks and shagging other people's husbands since 1928.

BADASS RATING: ★★

MORE ELECTRIC Es

ELISHA

Elisha Gray (1835–1901) was the enterprising engineer who developed the first telephone prototype. Many people would argue he actually invented the telephone, but was robbed of the credit for it.

BADASS RATING: ★★

ELISSA

Elissa Steamer (b.1975) is the first woman to smash it as a professional skateboarder.

BADASS RATING: ★★★★

ELSPETH

In 1983, **Elspeth Beard** (b.1959), an award-winning architect, became the first British woman to roar around the world on a motorbike when she was just twenty-four years old.

BADASS RATING: ★★★★

MORE ELECTRIC Es

ELWOOD

Elwood Widmer Etchells (1911–98) was an American boat designer and world championship sailor.

BADASS RATING: ★★

EMIL

Emil Fischer (1852–1919) was a Nobel Prize-winning chemist and scientist who discovered the class of sedative drugs used to treat insomnia, epilepsy and anxiety.

BADASS RATING: ★★★★

EMILY

Emily Davison (1872–1913), a fearless suffragette, died at the foot of a horse on her crusade to give women the right to vote.

BADASS RATING: ★★★★

MORE ELECTRIC Es

ERNŐ

Ernő Rubik (b.1944) the guy who invented the Rubik's Cube. Enough said.

BADASS RATING: ★★★★

ESTELLE

Estelle Winwood (1883–1984) was a quick-witted, no bullshit, feisty British actor whose career spanned almost eight decades.

BADASS RATING: ★★★★

ESTER

Ester Dean (b.1982) is the super-cool songwriter who has written for Rihanna, Beyoncé, Christina Aguilera, Katy Perry and Usher.

BADASS RATING: ★★★★

MORE ELECTRIC Es

ETHEL

Ethel L. Payne (1911–91), civil rights activist and tough-talking, trailblazing journalist, was hailed as the 'first lady of the black press'.

BADASS RATING: ★ ★ ★ ★ ★

EUPHEMIA

Euphemia Chalmers Millais (1828–97) was the woman at the heart of a famous Victorian love triangle, who outed John Ruskin as an oppressive and misogynist husband.

BADASS RATING: ★

EURIPIDES

A legendary Greek playwright, **Euripides** (484–406 BC) wrote over ninety-five plays, including the popularized *The Trojan Women*, and is renowned for breaking the mould of the traditional Greek tragedy by creating strong female characters.

BADASS RATING: ★ ★

MORE ELECTRIC Es

EVAN

Evan Williams (b.1972) is the whizz-kid and proud geek who co-founded Twitter, giving the world its own public soapbox in 280 characters.

BADASS RATING: ★

EVERARD

Everard Digby (*c*.1578–1606) was the ringleader of the bunch of pyromaniacs who tried to blast the shit out of the Houses of Parliament one cold November evening.

BADASS RATING: ★

EZRA

Ezra Freemont Kendall (1861–1910) was an A1 American actor, playwright and rare breed of comedian known for his rip-roaring monologues and parodies.

BADASS RATING: ★★

FANNIE

Will your little whippersnapper be creative, subversive and ready to make her mark? Then you could make her the namesake of the influential Victorian photographer, Fannie Johnston (1864–1952).

The first woman to be recognized as a prominent photographer, Fannie was regularly commissioned by magazines to take portrait shots and interiors of the famous and wealthy. From Alice Roosevelt's wedding to Edith Wharton's Parisian villa, Fannie's subjects showed she was trusted by some of the most powerful figures and families of her time. She was also honoured for her work capturing southern architecture and her photojournalism.

Fannie created rebellious self-portraits, often wearing typically male attire and adopting characteristically male poses. She questioned the roles and conventions of Victorian society and was not afraid to forge her own path. A champion for female empowerment, she encouraged women into the arts, especially as a means of supporting themselves. She curated exhibitions to celebrate other female photographers and made a career that spanned over sixty years.

BADASS RATING: ★★★★
A remarkable photographer, bohemian and badass.

FAZAL

Will your little soldier be dutifully devoted? Will he bravely persevere, no matter the situation? Then name him after Fazal Din (1921–45) – the gallant officer who managed to continue an attack on the enemy despite having a fatal wound in his chest.

Fazal served in Burma for the British Indian Army in 1945. He was just twenty-three when he led an attack on a Japanese bunker. During combat, he was fatally stabbed through the chest. With an injury like his, most people would give up and lie down to think of their loved ones and wait for death to descend, but not this guy. With the weapon in question protruding from his back, Fazal waited for the Japanese officer to withdraw it before tearing it out of his hands and killing him with it. He then attacked two more Japanese soldiers with the very same sword – and killed them – before crawling away from the scene to die.

Fazal was awarded the Victoria Cross for his bravery. Total badass.

BADASS RATING: ★★★
A bewilderingly brave and hard-as-nails hero who refused to surrender.

FERDINAND

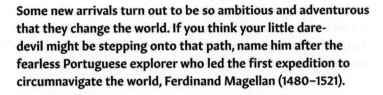

Some new arrivals turn out to be so ambitious and adventurous that they change the world. If you think your little dare-devil might be stepping onto that path, name him after the fearless Portuguese explorer who led the first expedition to circumnavigate the world, Ferdinand Magellan (1480–1521).

In 1519 Ferdinand kissed his wife and son goodbye, boarded a ship in the Armada De Moluccas and began a voyage that would make history. With 5 ships and 260 men under his command, Ferdinand and his crew sailed westwards from Spain to South America. Once across the Atlantic, Ferdinand found a passage through the southern Americas (now Chile) and set out to cross the strait that has come to bear his name. The journey was dangerous, with treacherous waters, and bitterly cold. The sailors on board grew weary and Ferdinand lost three of his ships. But after a long month of fighting uprising, hunger and scurvy, they were met by a vast ocean, which Ferdinand named the Pacific because of its apparent tranquillity.

BADASS RATING: ★★★
The mastermind of the first ever voyage to circumnavigate the world.

FIFI

Will your little snufflet be sassy and sage, and a natural when it comes to espionage? If so, you might want her to take the name of a glamorous and remarkable spy, Agent Fifi (also known as Marie Christine Chilver, 1920–2007).

Fifi was studying in Paris at the outbreak of the Second World War. When the Nazis invaded France, she was briefly imprisoned in an internment camp before making a cunning escape which involved nursing a wounded RAF soldier behind enemy lines, and then travelling back to London in his luggage. On arrival, the soldier in question demonstrated his gratitude for her lifesaving skills by outing her to MI5 as a potential enemy spy. Which she wasn't.

Once this was all cleared up, the Special Operations Executive were so impressed with her yarn-spinning skills that they hired her as a special agent, whose mission was to test potential secret agents and trick them into divulging secrets.

Fifi travelled throughout Europe, entrapping trainee spies, delivering reports on them and generally being a total badass.

BADASS RATING: ★★★★★
Full of derring-do, Fifi was hailed as trustworthy, courageous and 'one of the most expert liars in the world'.

FLORA

Would you like your daughter to be a tomboy, with mud on her face and twigs in her hair? Maybe you want her to chase her dreams, whatever obstacles lie ahead? Then make her the namesake of the woman determined to be equal to men in all pursuits – maverick army sergeant Flora Sandes (1876–1956).

In her childhood, Flora was the kid falling out of trees, clambering up mountains and handing out any necessary punches to local Yorkshire boys. She longed to become a soldier, but at that time in Britain, women were denied the right to serve in the army. So instead she gallivanted around the world on wild adventures, from Cairo to Canada and then across America. When the First World War broke out, she volunteered as a nurse with the Red Cross before joining the Serbian army (the only army that accepted women at the time) and swiftly moving up the ranks to sergeant major. She batted off battle wounds and was awarded medals for her extreme bravery, eventually joining the British troops in the trenches and becoming the only woman in the world to fight on the front line in the First World War.

A woman who could drink and smoke and gamble better than her male comrades, Flora continued to serve her country until she retired aged seventy.

BADASS RATING: ★★★★
A fiercely brave woman who battled against everything to achieve her dream of fighting alongside men as their equal.

FLORENCE

Smart, compassionate, strong-willed – just some of the attributes you might like your baby to have. And someone who had those qualities in spades was the celebrated medical pioneer, heroine and tour de force, Florence Nightingale (1820–1910).

Born into a wealthy family, Florence could have lived a life of luxury, but instead she fulfilled her dream of becoming a nurse. She shunned the then traditional methods of nursing, which included blood-letting and administering a concoction of mercury, arsenic and other less than desirable substances, in favour of a caring and holistic approach. Florence tended to basic human needs by championing good sanitation, warmth, nutrition and love.

While working in Crimea as a military nurse, she became known as the 'Lady with the Lamp' because she would visit soldiers at night, a small lantern in her hand lighting her way. And what began in army hospitals became a lifelong mission to improve patient care. Florence led a revolution in the world of medicine. On her return from the war in Crimea she wrote extensively about the dangers of unsanitary nursing practices. She installed hand-washing in hospitals across the globe and lobbied successfully to improve the methods of medical aid, becoming the first woman in history to be awarded the Order of Merit. She also fought for many social reforms, from abolishing harsh prostitution laws against women to employing a female workforce, and found time to write numerous accessible books on medical care.

BADASS RATING: ★★★★★
The legendary lifesaver, inspiration and forthright founder of modern nursing.

FLOYD

Will your little life nugget be entertaining, outlandish and a wizard with words? Then name him after the insightful and flamboyant bohemian writer, editor, radical socialist and feminist, Floyd Dell (1887–1969).

Born into poverty, Floyd left school to work at a candy factory where he was swiftly fired – probably for trying to start a revolt. He then joined the local newspaper and worked as a reporter, before leaving to edit a variety of socialist publications, including the revolutionary *Masses* magazine, known for its bang-on, radical politics. Anti-war, anti-government and an advocate of feminism, Floyd caused a riot writing articles that were pro-female sexual freedom and that championed women's liberation and the women's movement. The American government continually tried to stamp out the publication, eventually succeeding by accusing it of 'treason'.

Also a much-admired poet and novelist, Floyd's first novel *Moon-calf* became an instant bestseller. He wrote eleven more novels as well as poetry, plays and non-fiction.

BADASS RATING: ★★★★★
A lyrical leftist who gave the finger to the American bourgeoisie.

Fox

Will your little stork be curious and creative with ingenious ideas in abundance? Then name him after the artist, scientist, inventor and photography pioneer, William Henry Fox Talbot (1800–77).

While sketching landscapes on honeymoon in Italy, Fox first began to muse over an idea that he would later develop into the first ever photographic negative. By experimenting with placing objects onto photosensitive paper and exposing them to sunlight, Fox found a way to create imprints of natural images. In no time, the photographic negative, from which millions of prints could be made, was born.

From creating the first ever negative – a small postage stamp-sized picture of a window in his home in Lacock Abbey – to setting up a company that mass-produced paper prints, Fox opened up photography as an art form to everyone. A visionary and intellect, he was without a doubt the father of modern photography.

BADASS RATING: ★ ★ ★ ★
Fox's revolutionary innovations changed the way we see the world today.

FRANK

Want your puffling to live out his dreams at full throttle, speeding his way through life? Then name him after the badass who shrank the world and invented the jet engine, Frank Whittle (1907–96).

Obsessed with aviation from an early age, Frank applied to join the RAF but was deemed too short and 'not sporty enough' in his medical, so failed to get a place. Undeterred, he instead started at a technical training college where he demonstrated that while he might be on the puny side, he had far bigger balls than anyone else. It was there the idea for the Whittle unit (aka the jet engine) started whirring and purring in his mind. He drew up designs, but the British Air Ministry were less than supportive of his blueprint and dismissed it as unfeasible and too simple – and told him that it basically stood no chance.

Frank graciously shrugged off this feedback and thrust forward with his mission by setting up Power Jets Limited, securing £2,000 worth of funding from a guy willing to take a risk and singlehandedly turning his vision into a reality. The first prototype of the jet engine was built. On 15 May 1941, Frank's ambition took flight and his jet plane flew for a total of seventeen minutes across the Lincolnshire countryside, creating a legacy that has permanently altered human travel.

BADASS RATING: ★★★★★
The dude who rose up against all odds, took on the aviation establishment and changed the world.

FREDDIE

Some of us are born with killer looks. If you're sure your daughter's going to turn heads, you could name her after the beguiling beauty and Nazi-slayer, Freddie Oversteegen (b.1925).

At the outbreak of the Second World War, Freddie lived on a boat in the Netherlands with her family and together they smuggled Jews and others in need into the hold of their ship. Freddie also rode across town distributing fascist-fighting pamphlets and was determined to help with the war effort in every possible way,

When a man knocked at the door and invited Freddie to join the Dutch resistance, she went. She was taught to shoot, and then given a rifle and the mission to lure Nazis into the woods to meet their death. Freddie would sidle up to the unsuspecting, suggest they might like to go for a stroll. . . and once they arrived, instead of the nookie they were anticipating, Freddie would slink off and leave the Dutch army to blow their brains out.

BADASS RATING: ★
The woman who seduced Nazis to death.

FREDERICK

It takes a lot of pluck and daring to make the world a better place. If you fancy your son's chances of being a hero, name him after the badass who broke free from the shackles of slavery and became a symbol of emancipation in America, Frederick Douglass (1818–95).

Born as a slave on Maryland's eastern shore, Frederick worked tirelessly to educate himself and ultimately escape his captors. After several failed attempts, in 1838 Frederick boarded a train to Massachusetts cunningly disguised as a sailor. To fool the guards, he sported his best sea dog attire, borrowed a seaman's certificate and successfully made his way to freedom.

No longer bound by the chains of his oppressors, Frederick began a ceaseless campaign for abolition. He travelled the length of America, sharing his story. His autobiography became an instant bestseller and Frederick created a movement to try to eradicate slavery and racism in America and across the globe.

BADASS RATING: ★ ★ ★ ★ ★
An anti-slavery crusader who changed America.

FRIDA

Want to inspire your daughter to be an original – creative, free and empowered to write her own story? Then name her after the provocateur and rebel artist, Frida Kahlo (1907–54).

An indomitable spirit, Frida stood strong in the face of adversity. As a child she was bedridden by polo and developed a lifelong limp from complications, but this did not stop her from joining in a multitude of hardy sporting competitions, including lying smack-down as champion amateur wrestler.

When Frida was eighteen and training to be a doctor, she was in a serious traffic accident. As her bus collided with a car, she was on the wrong end of a steel handrail and it impaled her through the hip. Bedridden again, Frida turned to art to express her feelings and quickly rose to fame for her iconic self-portraits complete with proud monobrow, and imagery of monkeys, parrots and lush gardens.

A feminist and a visionary, Frida painted over 200 artworks in her lifetime. Exploring miscarriage, love, suicide and self-worth, she was never afraid to express herself or champion living life to the full. Viva la vida!

BADASS RATING: ★★★★★
An indomitable badass who boldly coloured the canvas of her life.

FRITZ

Are you growing a cheeky little rogue? Will he be brazen, bold and with the ability to outsmart just about everyone? Then take inspiration from the South African hellraiser who escaped every unlawful situation imaginable, Fritz Joubert Duquesne (1877–1956).

When Fritz discovered that the British army had killed his sister, imprisoned his mother and obliterated his home, he charged into Cape Town with a cohort of twenty men fired up to avenge his family. But before he could completely wreak havoc, he was arrested and sentenced to death. Rather than close the curtains, Fritz made up some story about secret South African codes, told them to the Brits 'discreetly' and was allowed to walk out, a free man, while the rest of his crew were lined up and shot.

Several years later, Fritz was getting tired of running in a bid to escape his own notoriety (and various criminal warrants.) So he faked his own death, wrote a moving obituary for the *New York Times* and snuck off to anonymity.

Until he was arrested, under his new guise, for a few more unlawful misdemeanours. This time, he pretended to be completely paralysed. He was spared jail and placed in a rather luxurious prison hospital where he kept up the act for TWO whole years before busting his way out the joint with epic style. First he dived through a window and then leaped from the roof and scaled a concrete wall before throwing himself over a massive iron-spiked fence and walking off into the sunset.

BADASS RATING: ★ ★ ★
An adventurer and freewheeler who later became a spy.

MORE FEARSOME Fs

FAYE

Faye Schulman (b.1919) was a Jewish partisan fighter and photographer who escaped the clutches of the Nazis, only to return to Poland to rescue her photography equipment.

BADASS RATING: ★★★

FIDEL

Fidel Castro (1926–2016) was the Cuban revolutionary, guerrilla fighter and longest-serving leader of Cuba.

BADASS RATING: ★

FRANCES

Frances Connelly was a badass woman who, mistaken for a man, voted in the British general election seven years before it was officially legal for women to vote.

BADASS RATING: ★★★

MORE FEARSOME Fs

FRANCIS

Francis Drake (1540–96), Britain's most feared sea dog, was the second man to circumnavigate the globe and is famous for leading the attack on the Spanish Armada.

BADASS RATING: ★★★

GABRIEL

Will you surround your future son with books and tell him tales of magical faraway lands? You could also spark his own imagination by making him the namesake of one of the greatest storytellers of the twentieth century, the Columbian author and journalist, Gabriel García Márquez (1927–2014).

The oldest of twelve children, Gabriel grew up listening to his grandmother's fables and family stories handed down over the generations. Since childhood he had longed to write a novel based on their house, the place where he had spent his formative years. Then one day, while driving his wife and kids to their annual holiday, the idea of how to begin the novel came to him. So he immediately turned the car around and drove home. He then sold the family car so they would have enough money for food and began feverishly writing. After eighteen months of writing daily and scraping by on the generosity of his local community, *One Hundred Years of Solitude* was born. It became an instant bestseller with fifty million copies sold worldwide. Castro liked it so much he bought Gabriel a house in Havana. In 1982, he was awarded the Nobel Prize in Literature. And when his mum learned of the honour, she kept it real by saying, 'That's great, son – now, can you fix my damn telephone?'

BADASS RATING: ★ ★ ★ ★
A true bohemian and one of the most significant writers of the twentieth century.

GENEVIEVE

Will your new bundle be gallant, generous and go around saving cities from destruction? Then it might be an idea to name her after the badass who saved Paris – Saint Genevieve (419–502).

Genevieve had a premonition that Attila the Hun (the savage, power-hungry, murdering marauder who spent a good part of 400 AD carrying out brutal attacks on every corner of the Roman Empire) was going to attack Paris. Everyone panicked and got ready to flee the city, but Genevieve told them to calm down and have a little prayer, and assured them that she would keep Paris safe. Naturally when Attila and his merciless army began yapping at the city walls, the Parisians started to doubt her. Fearing for their lives, a bunch of them got the hell out of there, but brave, bold Genevieve led the remaining civilians to just outside the city. Together they stood in unison in front of Attila's hungry horde and prayed. In no time the bunch of bandits approaching had dropped their weapons and fled.

A few years later, another tribe tried to attack Paris by blockading the city. The people quickly ran out of food and were just about to start chewing each other's arms when Genevieve coolly came to the rescue again. She snuck out of the city in a boat in the dead of night, begged nearby villages for rice and slunk back in with a boatload of it, saving her people from starvation.

BADASS RATING: ★★★★★
The fearless saint who saved Paris.

GEORGE

Was your baby overdue? Did the little tinker keep you waiting so long that medics had to intervene and physically kick him out of your lady parts? Then take inspiration from the tardy whizz-kid who accidentally solved the world's most unsolvable maths problems, George Dantzig (1914–2005).

While studying at Berkeley University, George rocked up to a statistics lecture just as it was closing. Full of remorse for the wild night before, he quickly scribbled down the homework before returning to his dorm to sleep off the rest of his headache.

A few days later he handed in his assignment. It was late, but that was nothing new, given George's timekeeping record; also, the work had seemed a little harder than usual, but he felt confident he had cracked it. It was only when his professor, Jerzy Neyman, read the answers and nearly fell off his chair that George realized something strange was going on. It turns out he'd mistaken some examples of notoriously unsolvable problems as homework – and solved them!

With brains like his, it is no surprise that George went on to achieve brilliance in the world of maths and science. He won a bunch of awards for his contributions and also created a famous algorithm that underpins all the scheduling systems for airlines, manufacturing, telecommunications and various other industries.

BADASS RATING: ★★★★
George Dantzig proved that lateness equals greatness!

Gertrude

Does your future child already have a taste for adventure? Will she also possess powers of great diplomacy? Then give her the namesake Gertrude Bell (1868–1926), embodiment of wanderlust, intrepid explorer, travel writer, anthropologist, archaeologist and kickass political advisor known for helping form modern-day Iraq after the First World War.

With unruly curls always pinned high on her head, a great love of cigarettes and a wild desire to learn, Gertrude blazed into the male-dominated institution of Oxford and showed them who was boss. She became the first woman ever to graduate with a degree in history – receiving first class honours, no less.

She shrugged off the idea of marriage and kids and instead began a voyage of exploration in the country now known as Iran. From honing her skills as a top mountaineer to photographing ruins or mapping out small areas of countryside, Gertrude feverishly journeyed across the Middle East. As she travelled, she shared her insights by publishing books detailing her adventures.

When the Ottoman Empire collapsed, Gertrude became instrumental in the construction of Iraq, literally drawing the borders by hand for the new country. With her sharp mind, gentle and accepting outlook, the Arabs adored her, and the new king insisted she become his sidekick and esteemed advisor. So she did and she kicked ass.

BADASS RATING: ★★★

A lioness with quiet determination and a sympathetic nature who smashed the patriarchy and changed the world.

GIACOMO

Will your son be quick-witted, with a thirst for knowledge and charming to boot? If so, why not take inspiration from the free-loving, free-thinking Italian adventurer, author and spy, Giacomo Casanova (1725–98)?

Giacomo flirted with as many careers as he did women. He was a lawyer, a violinist, a con man, a pimp, a dancer, a businessman, a diplomat, a spy and a politician, and is most famously known as the writer who boasted of the endless notches in his bedpost. But he was much more than just a horny libertine with a fondness for gambling, anything gourmet and ripping off gussets. Giacomo was smart.

Once, when he was imprisoned in the Doge's Palace as a consequence of his raucous lifestyle, Giacomo escaped from a lead cell. No one is quite sure how he managed this feat, but he served just half a day of a five-year sentence before slipping away unnoticed into the night. Badass.

BADASS RATING: ★ ★ ★ ★
A legend and a Lothario.

GIROLAMO

So, you're looking into the future and you see your newborn son... He's quick at maths and quicker at dealing cards... Hmm, better name him after the famous Italian polymath, Girolamo Cardano (1501–76).

An esteemed mathematician, doctor and astrologer, Girolamo had over 200 works published in his lifetime and was hailed as the father of modern algebra and inventor of the universal joint – a mechanical joint that connects stuff, for anyone wondering what the 'ell that is. He was also a compulsive gambler and often in need of some quick cash, which led him to write *Liber de Ludo Aleae*, the first book to systematically analyse probability. Girolamo basically realised he could clean up on the dicing table with some careful examination, and was kind enough to add a section at the back of his book on how to cheat at games of chance so he could help others to do so too.

Girolamo became notorious for reading horoscopes after doing a few for European royalty. He was so confident in his ability to predict the future that he told everyone his own death would be at the age of seventy-five. Legend has it that several days before his seventy-sixth birthday, Girolamo, still in fine health, necked a bottle of poison to ensure the truth of his own prophecy.

BADASS RATING: ★ ★ ★
Renaissance man and scientific pioneer.

GODIVA

Will your future filly be a compassionate, kind-hearted champion of the people? Then name her after the daring dissenter who stood up for the denizens of Coventry, Lady Godiva (d. *c.*1067).

When her husband, the earl of Mercia, decided to impose an additional and crippling tax on the citizens of the city, Godiva took matters into her own hands. She begged him to lift the harsh levies, but he refused. So she pleaded some more until he eventually agreed to do so – on the condition that she rode naked across the town.

The earl was pretty sure his wife would reject the challenge, but instead Godiva whipped off her skirt and skivvies, mounted her elegant white horse and galloped defiantly across the land, with only her long golden locks as a cover.

Thanks to Godiva's courageous canter, the earl was true to his word and lifted the taxes.

BADASS RATING: ★★★★
The peeress who ponied up for the people.

GRACE

You might feel that a demure name like 'Grace' won't fit your future daughter, who's bound to be strong, independent and super-sassy. But think again – you may not have heard of the pirate queen of Ireland who ruled the land and sea (and many hearts), Grace O'Malley (1530–1603).

A fiery redhead, Grace was born on the high seas into pirating royalty. As a young child she asked her father if she could accompany him on a voyage to Spain for some Catalan-style plundering, but he refused on account of her being a girl – her hair would get caught in the ropes of the ship. So Grace did what any other badass in her right mind would do – she lopped off her long locks and forced him to take her on the expedition.

When her father died, it was Grace rather than her brother who stepped up to run his sea-raiding empire. When her lover was murdered, she quickly brought her own form of justice to his killers. On another occasion, during an attack on Kinturk Castle, she observed that one of her sons was failing to charge with gusto. 'Are you trying to hide in my arse, the place you came out of?' she famously hollered.

Grace quickly gained a reputation as a champion marauder and fine Irish freedom fighter who took absolutely zero shit from anyone, including the queen of England.

BADASS RATING: ★★★★★
Extraordinary pirate queen and Irish legend.

GRAYSON

Fearless and flamboyant, mischief-making and imaginative: great qualities to aspire to. So why not name your bonny babe after the British artist who embodies all this and more – Grayson Perry (b.1960)?

Born in the county of Essex, Grayson's father left home when he was very young – an event that has had a major influence and impact on his work. He famously owns a rebel teddy bear called Alan Measles who has become his surrogate father as well as anarchist leader, fighter and also apparently an undefeated racing driver of the teddy bear world.

From living in squats in Camden Town with Boy George to hosting solo exhibitions across the globe, Grayson works with a mix of ceramics and textiles to chronicle life through his art. In 2003, he won the Turner Prize, controversially accepting the award alongside his wife and kids dressed as his legendary alter ego Claire – a forty-something woman who enjoys a ready meal in the evening and most likely lives on an estate of identikit Barratt homes.

BADASS RATING: ★★
A cultural icon who is not afraid to mock, mimic and question prejudice or gender boundaries.

GRETA

Will your little star be daring and discreet with skills in abundance? Then name her after the Scandinavian siren who ruled Hollywood while secretly working as a fascist-fighting undercover agent, Greta Garbo (1905–90).

A 1930s iconoclast, Greta was the highest-paid actor of her era. She was the queen of the silver screen, nominated for countless Academy awards, and in her heyday she could command a casual $150,000 a film. She was renowned for her privacy and elusive nature; unbeknown to Hollywood she also led a secret life embarking on countless dangerous espionage missions to gather vital intelligence about the Nazis.

She once slunk out of New York, dropping a lucrative film contract, claiming she needed to seek 'medical treatment'. Instead of checking into a prestigious hospital somewhere in Europe, Greta was in fact flying across the world to ambush the annual holiday of a blacklisted Hermann Goering comrade and elicit crucial information for MI6.

From tracking down millionaire Nazi sympathizers to leading negotiations with the king of Sweden in order to offer asylum to Danish Jews, Greta generally kicked fascist ass – all while leading a hugely successful acting career. What a legend.

BADASS RATING: ★★★★★
A majestic cult figure in Hollywood's Golden Age and intrepid secret agent.

GROUCHO

Do you reckon your baby's going to entertain you from the get-go? Maybe he'll be a super-slick, fast-talking, wisecracking comedian and star? If so, a good start would be naming him after Groucho Marx (1890–1977).

Master of wit, Groucho first skidded across the stage alongside his four siblings as part of the Marx Brothers, a pioneering act of slapstick, skit and song that had audiences roaring with laughter across the world. He was a mischief-making entertainer who went on to host his own hugely successful show. With his non-stop gags, horn-rimmed glasses and an enviable moustache, Groucho was known for his tomfoolery. He once performed a frantic Charleston dance across Adolf Hitler's grave, sporting his trademark beret. He was king of the quip: from 'I never forget a face, but in your case I'd be glad to make an exception,' to 'I've had a perfectly wonderful evening. But this wasn't it,' Groucho was a belly-laugh-inducing badass with balls.

BADASS RATING: ★★★★
Hailed as one of the greatest comedians to have ever lived.

GYDA

Who wouldn't like a Viking princess in the family? Especially one who knows her true worth... So how about naming your daughter after the Nordic royalty who unified Norway, Gyda Fairhair (*c*.852 AD)?

When offered the hand of King Harald of Norway, rebel princess Gyda shunned convention. She declared that she would only marry him if he first unified all the minor kingdoms of Norway. And because she had zero time for men with unruly mops of hair, she also insisted he swap his heavy-metal-inspired mane for a more clean-shaven crop. It took the Scandi warrior king ten long years of bloody battles, but he unified Norway in the name of love, took a razor to his face – and eventually, Gyda accepted his marriage proposal.

BADASS RATING: ★
A woman of principles who refused to settle for less.

GYPSY

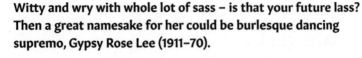

Witty and wry with whole lot of sass – is that your future lass? Then a great namesake for her could be burlesque dancing supremo, Gypsy Rose Lee (1911–70).

Turned into a show pony by her domineering mother, Gypsy spent her childhood as part of a troupe. But when her little sister ran off with a dancer, their company fell apart and Gypsy was left to support the family. So she defied her mother and began performing in burlesque clubs. Famous for inventing a new style of striptease that was as subtle and smart as it was sexy, Gypsy quickly became a star. She was known for her onstage banter and outlandish outfits, as well as commanding $10,000 a week for her shows.

Gypsy also had a sideline in saucy novels, among them *The G-String Murders*, proving that anything is possible – with a little naked ambition.

BADASS RATING: ★★★★★
The world's most famous stripper and queen of the bantz.

MORE GALLANT Gs

GALILEO

Galileo Galilei (1564–1642) was an Italian mathematician and astronomer who made a bunch of mind-blowing discoveries – from finding mountains on the moon's surface to spotting the four largest moons circling Jupiter.

BADASS RATING: ★★★★

GAVIN

Gavin Maxwell (1914–69), the high-drama, wilderness-loving otter champion and adventurer, secret agent and naturalist was never afraid to follow whatever path instinct told him to take.

BADASS RATING: ★★★

GERRY

Gerry Adams (b.1948) is the controversial Irish republican politician who started out as a revolutionary street activist and became a political leader.

BADASS RATING: ★

MORE GALLANT Gs

GIA

Gia Scala (1934–72), glamorous Italian-English siren of the silver screen, who was so badass it is believed that her ghost still haunts the hills of Los Angeles.

BADASS RATING: ★★

GLORIA

Gloria Steinem (b.1934) is a rebel journalist, businesswoman and leader of the modern feminist movement. She co-founded *Ms.* magazine and generally kicks ass.

BADASS RATING: ★★★★

GUIDO

Guido Fawkes (aka Guy Fawkes) (1570–1606) was the rebel anarchist and leader of the infamous Gunpowder Plot.

BADASS RATING: ★★★

MORE GALLANT Gs

GULAB

Gulab Kaur (1890–1941) bravely fought to liberate India from British rule; she joined the Ghadar movement, encouraging and inspiring many to stand up and fight for freedom.

BADASS RATING: ★★★★★

GUSTAVE

Gustave Whitehead (1874–1927) jumped off tall buildings with wings made from tissue paper in order to pursue his dream of flying, and arguably made history in the first manned aircraft.

BADASS RATING: ★★★★

HALINA

Will the newest member of your brood be zealous, born with mad athletic prowess and awe-inspiring sass? Then name her after the Polish world record-breaker, Olympic champion, writer and badass businesswoman, Halina Konopacka (1900–89).

With buns of steel and enough arm power to rival Popeye, Halina took up athletics while studying at Warsaw University. After a mere few months of training she broke the world record in the discus with a 34.15-metre throw. Halina then smashed it again at the 1928 Amsterdam Olympics, the first event where women could compete, winning the gold medal and setting her third world record of 39.62 metres. But hurling large circular discs through the air was not Halina's only talent. She was also a published poet, known for her bang-on feminist musings; she was one of Poland's best tennis players, was awarded a Silver Cross of Merit for helping the Polish government in exile and was dubbed Miss Olympia because of her breathtaking beauty. She also insisted on sporting a red beret at every tournament because why the hell not?

BADASS RATING: ★★★★★
In her 'retirement', Halina set up a skiing school, became a painter, designed her own clothing range and founded a boutique.

HARITA

Hope that your future daughter will be a high-flyer? Literally or metaphorically? You could name her after a woman who took to the skies – boundary-busting pilot and first woman to fly solo in the Indian Air Force, Harita Kaur Deol (1972–96).

Harita was just twenty-two when she flew high above clouds in an Avro HS–748, controlling an air force plane without a male co-pilot and marking a victory for women across India. Her demonstration flight was so impressive that one of the training officials remarked that she had more than outdone her male peers.

BADASS RATING: ★★★★★
A trailblazer who smashed through the patriarchy and made history.

HARRIET

Want to empower your little cub to be caring and courageous? Then make her the namesake of the almighty Harriet Tubman (1822–1913), the lioness who escaped enslavement and then kicked ass on countless missions to help others do the same.

Harriet was born into slavery in Maryland, America. Regularly whipped and beaten, she had a hole in her head as a result of an angry master's flying iron weight, but she refused to surrender to a life of imprisonment. Despite suffering lifelong pain and nausea from her head wound, she managed to flee the shackles of her captors and then went on to undertake some of the most fearless emancipation missions in history.

Harriet escaped her masters in 1849. Travelling under the cover of darkness and following the North Star, she eventually arrived in Pennsylvania to liberation. Armed with a new identity and a pistol strapped to her hip, Harriet then went back to help others escape. In just one year she led nineteen rescue missions, ushering people in the dead of night along the Underground Railroad, hiding out in safe houses or sleeping in ditches to avoid being seen.

She was pursued by authorities relentlessly. She was a wanted woman, but despite slave capturers offering a reward of $40,000 for her arrest, she was never caught.

Harriet guided over 500 people to freedom and inspired many more with her courage, bravery and ball-breaking badassery.

BADASS RATING: ★ ★ ★ ★ ★
The remarkable woman who walked the road to freedom and relentlessly risked her life to help others do the same.

HARVEY

Some people have mind-boggling courage when it comes to standing up for what they believe. If you admire folk like that, you could name your son after the gallant and groundbreaking gay rights activist and politician, Harvey Milk (1930–78).

Harvey refused to hide who he was. Disqualified from the navy for his homosexuality, he made his way to San Francisco. He set up a camera shop in the popular area of Castro and began to tirelessly campaign for reform of LGBT rights, eventually earning himself the moniker 'Mayor of Castro'.

He then battled against discrimination, death threats and hate to become the first ever openly gay American politician, winning a seat on the city's Board of Supervisors.

Harvey led an iconic LGBT civil rights movement in America, and his message was loud and clear – never be afraid to be who you are. 'If a bullet should enter my brain, let it destroy every closet door.'

BADASS RATING: ★★★★★
A man who succeeded in fighting for notable improvements in the civil rights of LGBT America.

HEDY

A woman of many talents: wouldn't it be great to know your daughter might be called just this? You could start by making her the namesake of the outrageous Hollywood star who also, on the side, worked on the technology that led to the invention of wi-fi. We're talking Hedy Lamarr (1914–2000).

Born in Austria, Hedy rose to fame as an actor and was known for speaking her own mind and not giving two pins about stripping naked in the name of art. When her first husband unleashed his controlling and abusive side, Hedy swiftly made her exit. Slamming the divorce papers on his desk and heading to Los Angeles via London, Hedy set the world ablaze on her own terms, from negotiating contracts to conquering Tinseltown as the star of the screen.

When the Second World War broke out, Hedy was determined to help America's efforts. In partnership with composer George Antheil, she casually invented a revolutionary new communication system for torpedoes – a system that underpins wireless technology today.

BADASS RATING: ★ ★ ★ ★ ★
The mega-smart powerhouse and actor who helped pioneer modern communications.

HELEN

You can achieve anything with hard work and a bit of badassery – what a message to give to your daughter! Put her on the right path by naming her after the humanitarian and first deaf-blind person to earn a degree, Helen Keller (1880–1968).

Diagnosed with 'brain fever' at nineteen months old, Helen soon began to lose the ability to see, hear and talk. But she refused to be silenced by her condition, and instead developed a way to express herself to her family through signs. After years of hard work, grit and determination, she could communicate well enough to gain a place at the Cambridge School for Young Ladies. By the time she was twenty-one, Helen had written an autobiography about her plight as a disabled woman. Her story began to spread across the world and she became an inspiration to many, including Mark Twain, who helped fund a place for Helen at Radcliffe College, Harvard. And so at the age of twenty-four, Helen graduated as a bachelor of arts.

BADASS RATING: ★★★★★
Champion of blind and deaf people, Helen took the bull by its horns and conquered her disability like a total BADASS.

HENRY

Will your little scallywag be a tireless adventurer and born leader? Then name him after the Welsh seafaring scoundrel responsible for kicking the Spanish out of large chunks of the New World, privateer Henry Morgan (1635–88).

A daring free spirit who fought as hard as he drank, Henry gathered a band of marauders from the far corners of Europe, building a fleet of 30 ships and 1,200 buccaneers. From soldiers to runaway slaves, with a few cutthroats and sociopaths thrown in for good measure, Henry's troop became the fiercest and most feared army of the west. They ruled the waves of the Caribbean, pillaging and looting along the way.

Henry was known for terrorizing Spanish merchant ships and destroying a large number of their settlements, which made him an unofficial hero to the English. Eventually, he retired to Jamaica to live on a life's worth of plundered riches.

BADASS RATING: ★ ★ ★ ★
A legendary buccaneer and namesake of a certain famous brand of spiced rum.

HERTHA

Will your little bean be inquisitive, smart and full of ideas? Then take inspiration from the fiery British engineer, mathematician and inventor, Hertha Marks Ayrton (1854–1923).

Born Phoebe Marks, teenage Hertha decided it was time for a rebrand and renamed herself after the ancient Germanic goddess Hertha. She won a place to study mathematics at Cambridge and became famous for her work on electrics and ripples.

A prolific inventor, Hertha had over twenty-six patents to her name. When the First World War broke out, she devised a fan that could suck up poisonous gases from the trenches, and 100,000 of them were sent to the front line.

BADASS RATING: ★★★★
The first woman to read a paper to the Royal Society, Hertha won the Hughes Medal in 1906.

HORATIO

Some names need little introduction: they're simply legendary. Go for it: name your son after the admiral who saved Britain's ass from Napoleonic invasion: Horatio Nelson (1758–1805).

A guy who clearly liked to live life on the edge, Horatio joined the Royal Navy aged twelve, despite suffering from severe seasickness. He quickly climbed the ranks from commander to captain and was finally promoted to admiral before the age of forty.

Famous for kicking the shit out of the French during the Napoleonic Wars, Horatio was the kind of leader who liked to play by his own rules. He regularly disobeyed orders from his superiors and once pretended that he couldn't see the signal to withdraw troops because he was looking through his telescope with his blind eye. What a joker. In fact, his bold ability to defy many of his seniors' commands actually helped the British triumph against the Spanish fleet on more than one occasion.

BADASS RATING: ★★★★
The brave British hero who upon his death was pickled in brandy. That is how you know you've made it.

HUGH

That's my boy: strong, adventuresome, a true survivor… If that's your secret daydream, why not name him after the man of the mountains who was mauled by a bear, left for dead but lived to tell the tale? We present Hugh Glass (1783–1833).

In the summer of 1823, Hugh was scouting for game along the banks of the Missouri river when he bumped into a grizzly bear. Looking out for her young, the furry animal launched herself at Hugh, lashing into his face, neck, back and arms and leaving him mortally wounded. Or so it seemed. When Hugh's fellow hunters found his body, they took one look at it, assumed he had already checked out and left. But death was not going to get her hands on Hugh just yet; this guy was not going down without a fight.

When he came to, Hugh set his broken leg with his bare hands, wrapped himself in a nearby bear skin and crawled some 200 miles back to civilization, surviving on maggots from his open wounds and the odd rattlesnake that crossed his path.

BADASS RATING: ★★★★
The hard-as-nails folk hero who took on the wilderness and won.

Humphry

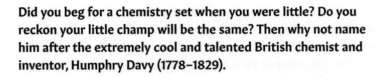

Did you beg for a chemistry set when you were little? Do you reckon your little champ will be the same? Then why not name him after the extremely cool and talented British chemist and inventor, Humphry Davy (1778–1829).

Humphry was the sort of kid who took messing about with a Bunsen burner on a rainy afternoon during a science lesson to the next level. After his father passed away, he became an apprentice to a famous surgeon, who, fuelling his inquisitive mind, gave Humphry access to a laboratory to perform endless explosive experiments.

The results were pretty impressive. First, Humphry invented the electric light. Then he invented a safety lamp for miners, which is more significant than it sounds. Prior to Humphry's handiwork, miners faced the daily excitement of potentially being blown to smithereens as they tunnelled underground guided by a naked flame with rising levels of methane in the air. Humphry's invention put an end to this daily dice with death. He also discovered nitrous oxide or laughing gas, which might come in handy when your little squidge makes his entrance.

BADASS RATING: ★★★★
A leading scientist of the eighteenth and nineteenth centuries.

HUNTER

So your son's gonna be smart, ambitious and ready to whip the world into a storm. Maybe he'll even live up to the reputation of rebel journalist and American author, Hunter S. Thompson (1937–2005). Name him Hunter and give it a try.

An anarchist, a rioter and boy of the South, Hunter lived outside the rules. He was banged up for a petty crime before he could finish school, and then kicked out the US air force for telling his superiors to 'get out of town' one too many times. From moonlighting as a sports journalist to becoming copy boy on a local paper before breaking stories in the big nationals, Hunter then blew through America, pen in hand, earning himself the title of Wild Man of journalism. He famously wrote *Fear and Loathing in Las Vegas*, a semi-autobiographical novel about two guys chasing the American dream on a feverish, drug-fuelled road trip, which has become a literary cult classic.

When he wasn't writing, Hunter spent his time in a hazy affair with sex, booze, hallucinogens and firearms. It is no surprise that his final act on earth was as large as the life he lived: Hunter's grand finale was to have Johnny Depp shoot his ashes from a cannon to the dulcet tunes of Bob Dylan's 'Mr Tambourine Man'. That, my friend, is leaving the world in style.

BADASS RATING: ★ ★ ★ ★
An icon of counterculture and badassery.

HYDNA

Does it feel like baby is performing aquatics in your abdomen? Is she swimming her way to stardom? Then name her after the Tom Daley of ancient Greece, known for her incredibly deep dives and mad long-distance swimming skills, which she ultimately used to save her country. We're talking Hydna of Scione (*c.*480 BC).

Given her father was a professional swimming instructor, Hydna was pretty much back-stroking her way across the Mediterranean Seas straight out of utero.

Around 480 BC the Persian king launched an attack on Greece. Defeated in early battles, the Greeks were in a state of panic. As enemy ships docked along the coastline preparing to advance further, a storm was brewing. Enter Hydna and her equally badass father, who saw an opportunity to kick some Persian ass. While the armies waited out the bad weather, they volunteered to swim across the violent waters and sneakily cut the moorings of the Persian vessels. Armed with knives to cut the anchors loose, the fearsome twosome set off on their mission, powering across 16 kilometres of rough seas. With no anchorage, the Persian fleet crashed together, some ships dramatically sank and the Greek army was able to strike back for victory.

BADASS RATING: ★★★★
The woman whose awesome aquatic abilities saved Greece from Persian rule.

HYPATIA

Will your little noggin be a numbers whizz who is ready to make herself heard? Then take inspiration from the famous Greek mathematician, spiritual leader and all-round badass who completely owned it in a male-dominated world: Hypatia of Alexandria (*c.*350–450 AD).

Bewitching, beautiful and with brains in abundance, Hypatia was a leading mathematician of her day. Known for her inventions in the fields of algebraic equations and astronomy, as well as her powerful public speeches, she has become the ultimate symbol of female freedom, intellect and reason.

Hypatia was head of the Neoplatonist School in Alexandria, regularly imparting her wisdom to reverent male academics. She was a queen who fought hard to live the life she wanted and refused to be silenced, even when it sadly led to her end.*

*Wondering what happened to Hypatia? She was brutally murdered by a band of barbaric monks who saw her as a threat to Christianity because she refused to convert from practising paganism and generally being true to her badass self.

BADASS RATING: ★★★★★
The greatest living mathematician of her time.

MORE HARDASS Hs

HANNAH

Hannah Arendt (1906–75) challenged the Nazis head-on and was made famous for her revolutionary ideas about totalitarianism.

BADASS RATING: ★★★

HARALD

Harald Fairhair (*c.*850–*c.*933 AD) was the ninth-century Viking ruler who rocked an outstanding head of hair and unified Norway in the name of love.

BADASS RATING: ★★★★

HARPER

Harper Lee (1926–2016) was the Pulitzer Prize-winning writer and author of *To Kill a Mockingbird*, a novel that dared to call out prejudice against race and class.

BADASS RATING: ★★★★

MORE HARDASS Hs

HARRISON

Harrison Okene is a Nigerian cook who, in 2013, survived for sixty hours trapped in an air bubble 30 metres (100 ft) below the sea.

BADASS RATING: ★★★

HAWA

Hawa Abdi (b.1947) is a Nobel Peace Prize-winning Somali doctor and human rights activist who built shelter for more than 90,000 refugees, saved countless lives, and has survived kidnapping and a brain tumour.

BADASS RATING: ★★★★★

HECTOR

Hector, prince of Troy (*c.*1250 BC), leader of the Trojan army, was known for possessing great courage, strength, nobility and loyalty. And for giving zero fucks.

BADASS RATING: ★★★

MORE HARDASS Hs

HENDRIX

Jimmy Hendrix (1942–70) was quite simply the world's greatest guitar player. Entirely self-taught and unable to read music, Hendrix was one of the most innovative and imaginative musical legends of our time.

BADASS RATING: ★★★★★

HERNANDO

Hernando (Hernán) Cortés (1485–1547) was a relentless Spaniard who arrived in Cuba, took on the Aztec empire, founded Mexico City and then discovered and conquered California.

BADASS RATING: ★★

IDA

Will your daughter have the courage to stand up for what is right and speak the truth for those who cannot? Then take inspiration from the invincible and incredible African-American civil rights activist whose campaign for equality changed the world, Ida B. Wells (1862–1931).

One morning Ida was riding the train to work when the conductor asked her to move along to the smoking carriage and give up her seat for a white woman. But Ida had purchased a first-class ticket and the conductor had messed with the wrong girl. She refused to move. Gripping her seat with steely force, Ida most likely responded with something like, 'Get the f— out of town with this oppressive bullshit. I'm going to sue your ass,' before hiring a lawyer and doing just that. On the first ruling, Ida won, and the train company was ordered to pay $500 in compensation. But once it got to the Supreme Court, the ruling was reversed.

    This fuelled an even bigger fire in Ida's belly, and she began writing and campaigning for racial equality. She set up her own paper, *Free Speech*, published numerous pamphlets and launched a global anti-lynching campaign that educated, empowered and ultimately reduced the number of racial attacks in America. From New York to London, Ida led an almighty crusade for equal rights for all.

BADASS RATING: ★ ★ ★ ★ ★
A fearless journalist, audacious activist and totally bona fide badass.

IRA

Will your son make a grand entrance into the world, like a thespian on opening night? Then name him after the theatrical sensation who punched prejudice in the face, Ira Aldridge (1807–67).

Ira first performed at the African Grove Theatre in New York, which was the first African-American theatre in the United States. But when it was burnt to the ground in a savage racist attack, Ira thought, 'To hell with this bigoted country,' and made his way to London, where parliament had abolished slavery.

His first gig was playing Shakespeare's *Othello* in Covent Garden, and his performance received glowing reviews. Ira went on to appear around the globe, as well as write his own plays and manage a production company.

BADASS RATING: ★ ★ ★ ★ ★
A legendary thespian of the nineteenth century, and the first black Shakespearean actor in England.

IRENA

Will your little babe be kind, caring and full of badassitude? Then name her after the heroic woman who relentlessly risked her life to save thousands of kids during the Second World War, Irena Sendler (1910–2008).

During the Second World War, Irena led a group of underground rebels who devoted themselves to rescuing children from the ghettos of German-occupied Warsaw and placing them in safe houses far away. The gang used a variety of tactics, from concealing those small enough underneath stretchers in the back of ambulances, to wheeling them away hidden inside trunks, or sneaking them out via sewer pipes. It was a highly dangerous operation, but saved many lives.

Eventually the Gestapo caught wind of their missions and Irena was arrested, tortured and interrogated before receiving the death sentence. But in a bold twist of fate, she escaped at the hands of her executioner, who unbeknown to her had been bribed by her quick-thinking comrades. Irena's shooting was faked and she was instead helped into hiding to see out the rest of the war.

BADASS RATING: ★★★★★
Irena saved more than 2,500 Jewish children from the clutches of the Nazis.

IRVING

Some people make it early; some people make it late. If you're sure your boy is going to be quick out of the starting blocks, name him after the 'Boy Wonder of Hollywood', Irving Thalberg (1899–1936).

A sickly child, bedridden with rheumatic fever, Irving was told by doctors that he would be lucky if he made it into adulthood. So he skipped college and went straight into world of business, determined to make his mark on the world before his time was up. By twenty years old he was a) still alive and b) running Universal Studios. By twenty-four he had co-founded his own media company and turned it into the world's most profitable studio. From Joan Crawford to the Barrymores, Irving launched careers, made stars and oversaw the production of an epic 400 films before his death aged thirty-seven.

BADASS RATING: ★ ★ ★ ★ ★
The producer who survived childhood illness to become a prince of Hollywood.

ISAAC

Will your son be fearless and flamboyant with zero sense of danger? Then name him after the most famous lion-tamer of the nineteenth century (and really ever), Isaac Van Amburgh (1811–65).

Known for his outrageously daring shows, Isaac would dive head first into a metal cage, dressed in nothing more than a Roman toga, and then proceed to taunt and tease his pride. Performing on the backs of lions, leopards and tigers was just part of his show; he would also re-enact scenes from the Bible, sometimes inviting a baby lamb or even a small child to join him. For his grand finale, Isaac would cover himself in blood and stick his head into a lion's mouth.

Adored (and quite possibly stalked) by Queen Victoria – she attended his show seven times in one season – Isaac was asked if he would pose with his cats in a painting for her personal collection. Which of course he did.

BADASS RATING: ★★★★
Confident and cocky, with every bone in his body made out of pure courage.

Isabel

Now, here's a name for you: Isabel Cristina Leopoldina Augusta Micaela Gabriela Rafaela Gonzaga de Bragança e Bourbon. Why not go with that? (Just kidding.) But if you're growing a little princess, the shorter version could work very well. Princess Isabel (1846–1921) was a bright, independent and rebellious royal who freed every slave in Brazil.

Heir to the Brazilian throne, Isabel first took up regency when her mother and father went on an official tour of Europe. With her parents on the other side of the world, quaffing grape juice in Bordeaux and enjoying an extended jolly, Isabel began a quiet campaign to end slavery in her country. First she created and signed a new act to free all slave children born after that date. Then a few years later, when her father was hurried out of the country due to ill health, Isabel once again became regent – and this time pushed through a law that completely abolished slavery in Brazil.

BADASS RATING: ★★★★
The wilful royal who, when her parents were out of town, used her power to end enslavement for her people.

Isadora

Will your little twinkle-toes prance her way into the world, spinning it around her little finger? Then maybe you should name her after the acclaimed American dancer, ballet rebel and mother of modern dance, Isadora Duncan (1877–1927).

Isadora took one long look at the world of classical ballet and declared that stiff pointe shoes, tight corsets, rigid tutus and restrictive movements were OUT – and that creative, self-expressive, free-flowing and natural movements were IN. She encouraged dancers to perform barefoot and challenged outdated performance styles.

And it was not just in the world of dance that Isadora shunned conventions. She protested against the institution of marriage, and so bore all her children out of wedlock; and as a proud communist, she refused to be silenced even when it meant her American citizenship was revoked.

BADASS RATING: ★★★
Dancer, adventurer, feminist and also a champion of free love, Isadora spearheaded the development of modern dance.

MORE INVINCIBLE Is

ILAN

Ilan Shamir (b.1951) is a tree-hugging, lumber-loving nature warrior who has planted more than 100,000 trees and spent his life celebrating and protecting them.

BADASS RATING: ★★★

IMMANUEL

Immanuel Kant (1724–1804) was a hugely influential German philosopher, who inspired Einstein and many others.

BADASS RATING: ★★★

INDIRA

Indira Gandhi (1917–84) smashed the patriarchy to become the first and only female prime minister of India.

BADASS RATING: ★★★

MORE INVINCIBLE Is

IRIS

Iris Murdoch (1919–99), an affectionate, witty, brainy-as-hell writer and philosopher, won the Booker Prize and the hearts of readers with her fiction.

BADASS RATING: ★★★

IRVINE

Irvine Welsh (b.1958) is a controversial Scottish author who has written a bunch of completely rad novels, most famously *Trainspotting*.

BADASS RATING: ★★★

IRWIN

Steve Irwin (1962–2006) was the cool, crazy and totally bonkers crocodile hunter who made a career out of wrestling the most dangerous animals in the world for light entertainment.

BADASS RATING: ★★★★

JACK

Your little buster may not end up a boxer, but you're probably hoping he'll be a heavyweight who attacks life with plenty of punch. So why not name him after the record-breaking African-American boxer with the best counter-punch in history, Jack Johnson (1878–1946)?

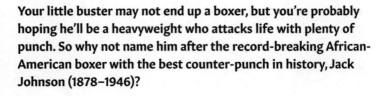

Apart from being one of the greatest boxers that ever lived, Jack's life outside the ring earns him the crown of most legendary badass in this book. Flash, flamboyant and living life in the fast lane, Jack owned a pet leopard, his own jazz band, a nightclub in Chicago and a dazzling collection of gold teeth. He was partial to bullfighting; he was a star of the stage and was also a secret agent for the US in the First World War.

He was locked up for seven years for trying to bang his future wife (she was white, he was an ex-slave, the government were racist assholes) but during that time Jack did not just kick back – he invented and patented his own version of the wrench instead. This guy!

BADASS RATING: ★★★★★
The heavyweight boxing champion who smashed through the colour barrier and lived a life of extreme badassery.

JACKSON

Want to inspire your son to stand up tall for what he believes? Then make him the namesake of the hellraising activist and filmmaker who's on a mission to stamp out sexual violence, Jackson Katz (b.1960).

A high-school jock and die-hard feminist, in the 1980s Jackson was the first man to graduate from the University of Massachusetts Amherst with a degree in women's studies. Since then has devoted his life to teaching men to take responsibility for stopping sexual assault. With a powerful voice, Jackson's bold and blunt crusade has taken him to pretty much every institution across the globe where he has inspired men to step up and help the world stop sex crimes against women.

BADASS RATING: ★★★★★
The activist making violence against women a man's issue.

JACQUELINE

Does it feel like the baby in you tummy is performing aerobatic manoeuvres to rival the Red Arrows? Then how about naming her after the queen of speed who somersaulted, span and soared across the skies, Jacqueline Cochran (1906–80)?

Jacqueline still holds more distance and speed records than any other pilot in living history. She was the first pilot to fly above 6,000 metres without an oxygen mask; the first pilot to make a blind landing; the first woman to fly a bomber across the Atlantic. Jacqueline broke the sound barrier and became the first female to compete in the transcontinental aeronautical race called the Bendix Trophy, which she then went back to win the following year.

When Jacqueline wasn't zipping through the clouds and showing the aeronautical world who was boss, she found time to run for Congress, launch a successful cosmetics company, design a line of aerodynamic underwear* and give a shitload of her wealth to charity.

* The pants part might not be 100 per cent true, but if she could have, she would have…

BADASS RATING: ★★★
A brave, bold, record-breaking badass who reached for the stars and landed on the moon.

JANE

Will your little monkey be an eco-warrior with gorilla-sized dreams? Take inspiration from the groundbreaking British environmentalist and world-saver, Jane Goodall (b.1934).

As a young child, Jane had always dreamed of living with wild animals and going on adventures; so when she finished school, she picked up the phone, dialled the number of a well-known palaeoanthropologist and wangled her way to joining him on his next trip to Africa. From Kenya to Tanzania, Jane observed and studied chimpanzees. Living among them, she was able to make revolutionary discoveries about their behaviour and intelligence.

BADASS RATING: ★★★★★
A humanitarian, a planet-protector and one of the world's most celebrated primatologists.

Jann

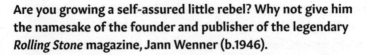

Are you growing a self-assured little rebel? Why not give him the namesake of the founder and publisher of the legendary *Rolling Stone* magazine, Jann Wenner (b.1946).

The offices of *Rolling Stone* in the 1970s were enough to make an episode of *Mad Men* look like a bunch of straightedges at a sobriety convention. The photo department dealt white powder to employees at the back of the dark room, bottles of vodka were downed before breakfast and the staff of the magazine quite literally lived the sex, drugs and rock 'n' roll lifestyle that they wrote about. And at the helm was Jann, a mastermind, radical and pioneer of a new form of journalism.

BADASS RATING: ★★★★
The guy who invented the term 'to give zero fucks'.

JEANNE

Can you feel the burning in your belly to be that of a little lioness, ready to stamp her own form of justice on the world? Then take inspiration from the French princess turned privateer, Jeanne de Clisson (1300–59).

It didn't pay to mess with Jeanne. When the king of France mistook her husband for a traitor and beheaded him, Jeanne swore blind vengeance. Leaving her castle in a cloud of smoke, she concealed herself in the fog of the English Channel and began a reign of terror against the French. Transforming herself from noblewoman to swashbuckling pirate, Jeanne led the Black Fleet, a band of Frog-slaying buccaneers famous for charging at French lairds with an axe and then throwing their decapitated bodies out to sea.

BADASS RATING: ★★★★
A queen of the high seas who handed out her own form of retribution.

JEREMY

Will your little star rise up to make this world a fairer place? Then name him after Labour Party maverick and socialist hero, Jeremy Corbyn (b.1949).

Man of the people, Jeremy was the anti-war, anti-austerity, anti-privatization underdog who stormed the Labour Party to take up its reins in 2015. From owning the pyramid stage at Glastonbury to working on the streets of Islington, Jeremy is the unassuming leftist hero. He has held his seat in parliament for over thirty-six years, and has inspired a new generation to engage with politics. Sporting a quality beard, Jeremy still wears his mum's jumpers, doesn't own a car and has the lowest expense claims of any MP.

Hailed as Saint Jezza, and seen as the antidote to the many Etonians perched on the pews of parliament – whether loved or loathed, no one can deny that he is trying to make the world a better place.

BADASS RATING: ★★★★★
Rank outsider and ALL-ROUND BADASS.

JESSE

Will your little boy enter the world at breakneck speed? Then name him after the record-smashing sportsman who swiftly cut Hitler down to size, Jesse Owens (1913–80).

Jesse, an African-American athlete of field and track, was so insanely fast that at one point he held the world record for every single sprint distance in human history. Unbeaten for twenty-five years in the long jump, Jesse is also fondly remembered for making Der Führer look like a dick at the 1936 Olympics when he took home four gold medals, smashed two world records and became a legend in Berlin. After Jesse left the Germans for dust in the 100m sprint, Hitler apparently stormed out of the stadium. In your face, Adolf.

BADASS RATING: ★★★★★
Human dynamite.

JOAN

Will your daughter have special powers? Then name her after the courageous warrior who led French troops to victory, Joan of Arc (1412–31).

Born during the Hundred Years War, Joan was a poor and illiterate French girl who became a national hero. The story begins when one day, Joan was casually hanging out washing in her garden when a force from heaven appeared before her, imploring her to help drive the English out of France. So off Joan galloped to the court of Charles VII to share her vision. It takes a true badass to march up to a king and persuade him to hand over the military reins to a sixteen-year-old girl he has never met before. But that is exactly what she did. And a short while later, an armour-clad Joan led the French army to a breathtaking victory at the besieged town of Orléans. #GOALS

BADASS RATING: ★ ★ ★ ★ ★
A national heroine of France and poster girl for extraordinary courage.

JOE

Want to inspire your son to persevere in the face of adversity? Then name him after the mountaineer who was left for dead in the Peruvian Andes but crawled his way back to civilization: Joe Simpson (b.1960).

In 1985, Joe and his pal Simon Yates were descending the Siula Grande, an ice-covered and almost completely vertical mountain, when a blizzard struck. The pair were roped together but, dazed by the extreme weather, Joe found himself dangling off the edge of a cliff, 45 metres above the ground with nothing more than a rope and his buddy Simon to stop him from plummeting to his death. Simon struggled for twelve hours to pull Joe back to safety, but conditions were beyond tough; the men were exhausted, so eventually Simon cut the rope to save himself.

First, Joe survived falling off the edge of the cliff. Then, with a broken leg and no food or water supplies, he survived a gruelling four-day journey back to base camp.

BADASS RATING: ★★★★★
One of Britain's best-known explorers, who proved that if your balls are big enough, you can literally survive anything.

JONAH

Will your kid be unstoppable? Then name him after the rugby superstar who could run faster than a Ferrari loaded with rocket fuel, Jonah Lomu (1975–2015).

Born in New Zealand and a player for the All Blacks, Jonah was a tour de force of the rugby world who could run 100 metres in 11 seconds flat. Despite had a rare kidney disorder that required several bouts of major surgery, Jonah still completely owned the rugby pitch. He was the youngest-ever All Blacks player in the 1995 World Cup, and will forever be remembered as one of the greatest players of all time.

BADASS RATING: ★★★★
One of rugby's greatest badasses.

Jonas

Want to inspire your little one to have boundless curiosity and the courage to make his dreams reality? Then name him after the unconventional scientist and all-round rad human being who developed the cure for polio, Jonas Salk (1914–95).

In 1955 Jonas became a global hero for creating a vaccine to prevent polio. This milestone had been seven years in the making, and underwent one of the biggest ever clinical trials in America. Jonas was also part of the crew that developed the flu vaccine, and in the later part of his life carried out pioneering research in the hope of developing a vaccination against AIDS.

BADASS RATING: ★★★★★
A knight in a white coat.

JØRGEN

Want to inspire your son to live life at full throttle? Then name him after the Danish adventurer who blazed into Iceland and crowned himself king, Jørgen Jørgensen (1780–1841).

Jørgen's idol was Captain Cook, which is a pretty good starting point for his story. Born in Copenhagen to a clockmaker, by the time he came to declare himself king he had already sailed across the globe, colonized Tasmania, assisted Napoleon in an attack on the British, escaped execution and run up enormous debts in London. Fleeing financial ruin, Jørgen sailed to Iceland to trade, but when officials refused his services, he staged a coup.

Jørgen ruled Iceland for some months before the British intervened and banged him up. They later freed him, made him a spy, hailed him a hero, decided to imprison him again and then transported him to Tasmania to live as a convict. Oh, the irony. He was later freed and declared a national hero again. You can see where this is going...

BADASS RATING: ★★★★
A man of many hats with a life story that reads like fiction.

JULES

Got a little gymnast somersaulting in your stomach? Is your future spawn set to become a high-flyer? Then why not name him or her after the death-defying stuntman who took aerial acrobatics up a level by inventing the flying trapeze, Jules Léotard (1838–70).

How *does* one invent the flying trapeze, I hear you ask? Well, it all began at the swimming pool. Jules started experimenting above his dad's pool by tying a couple of ropes to the ceiling and swinging from the bar like a monkey. Presumably, this was the perfect outlet for a stressed-out solicitor – yep, this daredevil gymnast was also a qualified lawyer.

After some time practising his tricks, Jules unveiled his grand act at the Cirque Napoleon in Paris in 1859. Audiences gasped in awe as he somersaulted between five different trapezes with only a couple of mattresses casually placed on the floor to break his fall. And to show off his muscular physique while swinging from the rafters, Jules also invented a snug one-piece we now know as the leotard.

BADASS RATING: ★★★★
The lawyer who ran away to join the circus.

JULIAN

Want to inspire your future son to always tell the truth? Then give him the namesake of the Australian cypherpunk who waged a war on secrecy, Julian Assange (b.1971).

Passionate and pertinacious, Julian began hacking as a teenager under the name Mendex, meaning nobly truthful. By 2006 he had founded WikiLeaks, a website dedicated to exposing censored information involving war, spying and corruption by hacking into confidential databases. Pursued by authorities across the world, a wanted a man and a cyber rogue, Julian liberated scandalous state secrets through sheer geek power.

BADASS RATING: ★★★★
Computer nerd-cum-hacktivist.

JULIANE

Is your baby a miracle? Then name her after the sole survivor of a deadly plane crash, Juliane Koepcke (b.1954).

Divine intervention or not, it takes an extreme kind of badass to survive a full-on disaster – especially when you're only seventeen.

On Christmas Eve in 1971, Juliane was on a plane to Peru when lightning struck. Still strapped to her seat, she plummeted from the sky for two miles before landing in the heart of the Amazon rainforest. Every single person on board that flight died. Except Juliane, who picked herself up, brushed off the aluminium shards and began walking to safety. Despite a broken collarbone, a gaping hole in her arm, zero supplies and the wholly appropriate trekking attire of a mini-dress and sandals, Julianne crawled through the jungle for ten days. Delirious with concussion, her wound now infested with maggots, Julianne eventually stumbled across two locals who helped guide her home.

BADASS RATING: ★★★★★
The woman who fell to earth, gave death the finger and took bravery to another level.

JULIE

Will your daughter be born with a burning desire to tell stories? Then take inspiration from the trailblazing African-American film director, Julie Ethel Dash (b.1952).

In January 1992, Julie made history with the release of her narrative film, *Daughters of the Dust*. Despite receiving rejections from many of the Hollywood executives she approached, Julie persevered and eventually it was produced in collaboration with the Corporation for Public Broadcasting.

A breathtaking drama, *Daughters of the Dust* became the first ever film to hit mainstream cinema that had been directed and produced by an African-American woman. It went on to win a bunch of awards, including the Sundance Film Festival award for excellence in cinematography, leading the way for a future generation of artists. The film also famously inspired Beyoncé's *Lemonade* video – from one epic badass to another...

BADASS RATING: ★ ★ ★ ★
African-American film director who made one of the most important cinematic achievements of the twentieth century.

JUNKO

Want to inspire your daughter to challenge herself? Then name her after the Japanese alpinist and first female to reach the summit of Mount Everest, Junko Tabei (1939–2016).

People told Junko that Everest was no place for a woman, and that she should stay at home with her children. Good job she told them where to stick it. In 1975, Junko led an all-female expedition to Everest. She survived being buried under an avalanche and crushed by her teammates before thankfully being rescued by Sherpas from the neighbouring camp. Junko persevered, battling sub-zero temperatures on her gruelling voyage; in just twelve days she reached the summit, making history.

If Everest wasn't enough, Junko then went on to become the first woman to climb all of the Seven Summits by conquering the highest point in every continent.

BADASS RATING: ★★★★★
A fearless adventurer and all-round powerhouse.

MORE JOYOUS Js

JAMES

James Naismith (1861–1939) was the guy who invented basketball in 1891. Score!

BADASS RATING: ★★★★

JAN

Jan Sobieski (1629–96), known as the king who saved Europe, led the biggest ball-stomping cavalry in history.

BADASS RATING: ★★★

JETHRO

Jethro Tull (1664–1741) was an inventor and pioneer of some impressive horse-hoeing husbandry (a seed drill), which back in the day totally revolutionized farming. So goddamn badass a British rock band took his moniker.

BADASS RATING: ★★

MORE JOYOUS Js

JIM

Jim Lovell (b.1928) was the Apollo 13 commander and hero who safely brought his crew back to Earth after an oxygen tank exploded inside their rocket.

BADASS RATING: ★★★★★

JOHN

John McEnroe (b.1959), the bad boy of tennis and former world no. 1, was notorious for his on-court cusses, outbursts, racquet-throwing and basically giving zero f*cks.

BADASS RATING: ★

JOSEPH

Joseph Gallieni (1849–1916) was the French general who came out of retirement to save Paris's ass from being whipped by the Germans; he fought them off with an army of taxi cabs.

BADASS RATING: ★★★

MORE JOYOUS Js

JOSEPHINE

Josephine Butler (1828–1906), feminist and social welfare warrior, reformed the Contagious Diseases Act, which had stripped poor women of their legal rights.

BADASS RATING: ★★★★

JOSHUA

Joshua Slocum (1844–1909) was the first man to sail singlehandedly around the world.

BADASS RATING: ★★★★

KARL

Does your newborn son look like he is deep in thought? Then give him the namesake of the radical and revered philosopher who started a revolution, Karl Marx (1818–83).

The father of socialism, Karl was born in Prussia and lived most of his life in poverty, trying to make sense of the corrupt, dishonest, avaricious world. A legend for calling out greed, Karl waged a war against capitalism, fought for the abolition of oppression and exploitation, and inspired an everlasting rebellion.

He famously co-authored *The Communist Manifesto*, the most influential political document in the world, and his radical writings saw him kicked out of Germany, France and then Belgium before he eventually settled in England. A dude who was earnest, determined and with so much badassery it is still squirting from his veins six feet underground.

BADASS RATING: ★★★★★
The most influential and BADASS figure in human history.

KATE

Will your new human be kind, compassionate and willing to travel to the ends of the earth to help those in need? Then name her after the British nurse who dared to find the cure for leprosy, Kate Marsden (1859–1931).

In February 1891, Kate set out on a mission to find a medicinal herb thought to cure leprosy, or at the very least to relieve the symptoms. Kate travelled by train, then sledge, then horse to the depths of Siberia. She struggled through marshes, bogs and pitch-black forests, and fought off bears before eventually arriving at the leper colonies of Yakutsk where the herb was said to grow. Kate returned home some eleven months later, samples in hand, ready to kick leprosy's ass.

BADASS RATING: ★★★★
A brave Victorian who undertook a marathon journey across northern Asia to help the plight of others.

KATHERINE

Will your little noggin be born with a knack for numbers? Then name her after the African-American aeronautical trailblazer whose calculations forever changed the world, Katherine Johnson (b.1918).

Katherine was an ace at arithmetic and adored maths from a young age. Recognizing this, her father hunted down a school that would accept a black woman from West Virginia, and together they drove 120 miles a day to make sure Johnson got the education she deserved.

When NASA advertised for women to do the job of a 'computer', doing calculations for their space programme, Johnson joined the crew. But she did more than just churn out numbers. She did the complex equations that pioneered some of the world's greatest achievements in space.

And Johnson demanded to be heard. When women were excluded from all meetings and briefings, she marched up to the old boys and insisted on an invitation. She questioned why and how decisions were made and she made damn sure she had a place at the table. In no time, Johnson was one of NASA's most trusted mathematicians.

From calculating the flight path for the first American space mission to nailing the vital computations that put the first man on the moon, Johnson blazed an earth-shattering trail of badassery in the world of space flight.

BADASS RATING: ★★★★
A brainy badass who fought the system to follow her dreams.

KATIA

Want to inspire your daughter to follow her passion? Then name her after the fearless French volcanologist who spent her life ascending fiery mountains, Katia Krafft (1942–91).

In awe of their power and beauty, Katia spent her life documenting volcanoes. With extreme badassery and camera in hand, and accompanied by her equally hardcore bae, Katia filmed volcanic eruptions. She would stop at nothing to get the perfect shot, clambering up to the edge of each crater, often feet away from 1,000-degree lava, ducking molten missiles and with death so close she most likely felt his breath on her neck.

When Mount Pinatubo showed signs of imminent eruption, it was Katia who insisted on the evacuation of the entire area, her footage of previous disasters swaying those in doubt. A lifesaver, a pioneer and a fearless adventurer who followed her dreams.

BADASS RATING: ★★★★★
It doesn't get more badass than storming up a hot, fiery lava-spewing volcano.

KATRÍN

Want to encourage your daughter to make the world a better place? Then make her the namesake of Katrín Jakobsdóttir (b.1976), the environmentalist, Icelandic politician and brilliant human being.

Katrín is leader of the Left-Green Movement and became prime minister of Iceland at just forty-one years old in 2017. A woman on a mission for change, Katrín is driving a crusade against global warming. She has vowed to make Iceland completely carbon-neutral by 2040, and has a bunch of other banging ambitions and policies that make her one of the most badass prime ministers that has ever lived. Fact.

She also once had a side career in sprinting across the background of music videos, because she's just that kinda powerhouse.

BADASS RATING: ★ ★ ★ ★
Eco-warrior, leftist rebel and not your average politician.

KEIKO

Will your future daughter be small but mighty? Then name her after the pint-sized martial arts maestro who judo-flipped her way to become the highest-ranking female in history, Keiko Fukuda (1913–2013).

The granddaughter of a samurai and jiu-jitsu master, Keiko had learnt how to pin-lock opponents before she was even out of her mother's arms. When judo, a new form of martial art, began to emerge in Japan, Keiko was one of its first students, shunning an arranged marriage in favour of training to be even more badass.

Keiko quickly became a fifth-level black belt (which is already pretty damn hardcore), but could not progress any further because the judo institute would not allow women to do so. So Keiko campaigned for them to drop their sexist practices, and won. At the age of ninety-eight, Keiko was awarded the tenth dan, Judo's highest rank – tell that to your grandma!

BADASS RATING: ★★★★★
One strong woman who lived life by the rule, 'Be a good human.' Damn straight.

KEIR

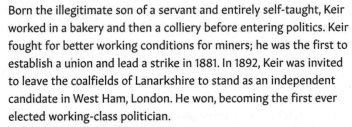

Want to inspire your son to rise up and forge a better world? Then name him after the working-class hero and founder of the Labour Party, Keir Hardie (1856–1915).

Born the illegitimate son of a servant and entirely self-taught, Keir worked in a bakery and then a colliery before entering politics. Keir fought for better working conditions for miners; he was the first to establish a union and lead a strike in 1881. In 1892, Keir was invited to leave the coalfields of Lanarkshire to stand as an independent candidate in West Ham, London. He won, becoming the first ever elected working-class politician.

He shunned the stiff suits of parliament, always sporting his trademark tweed, and from the corridors of Westminster he began a movement that would form the Labour Party. Keir was a tireless campaigner for the working class, for women and for a better world.

BADASS RATING: ★★★★★
The man who changed the political landscape of Britain forever.

Khutulun

Will your little warrior be strong, independent and invincible? Then name her after the wrestler princess who was undefeatable in the ring, Khutulun (*c.*1260–*c.*1306).

Any descendant of Genghis Khan is going to be pretty damn hardcore, and his great-granddaughter Khutulun was no exception. A powerful athlete, in archery she could shoot a bullseye with her eyes shut; she had great skill in commanding horses; and in the wrestling ring she was unbeatable.

Khutulun had many suitors and challenged each one to a wrestling match, announcing that if they could beat her, she would marry them. She persuaded each admirer to bet his entire collection of horses on the fight. Of course, Khutulun never lost. Delivering almighty dropkicks and out-fighting any eligible bachelor, she marked her place in history as one of Mongolia's greatest warriors.

BADASS RATING: ★★★★★
The rebel royal who never lost in battle – and ended up with a lot of horses.

KITTY

Will your little champ be born to run? Then name her Kitty after the woman who smashed the patriarchy to become the first to run the Boston marathon, Kathrine Switzer (b.1947).

Banned from entering the Boston Marathon because it was 'physically impossible' for women to run that distance, Kitty decided to prove the race organizers wrong. She trained, racking up impressive thirty-one-mile runs, proving she was more than capable, and entered the race illegally in 1967. On seeing a woman casually jogging along, one of the officials charged at her screaming, 'Get the hell out of my race!' Being a total boss, Kitty leapt backwards as another competitor rugby-tackled him to the ground, enabling her to run on and valiantly cross the finish line in four hours and twenty minutes – a victory for womankind.

Five years later, thanks to Kitty's courage to run, women were officially allowed to compete in the Boston Marathon. Kitty went on to campaign for the inclusion of the women's marathon in the Olympic Games. And, of course, smashed it again.

BADASS RATING: ★★★★
A groundbreaking athlete who revolutionized sports for women.

Krystyna

Will your daughter possess extreme courage? Then name her after the award-winning wartime secret agent, Krystyna Skarbek (1908–52).

After fleeing her native Poland at the outbreak of the Second World War, Krystyna was recruited by British intelligence to work as a spy. Determined, mesmerizingly charming and with nerves of steel, she skied her way into Poland, parachuted down into France and smuggled vital intelligence back into Britain – rolled up inside her long-sleeved gloves.

With her quick thinking and calm demeanour, she won her release from various arrests and once secured her freedom by pretending to be the niece of Field Marshal Montgomery. Another time, during a particularly harsh interrogation, she bit her tongue so hard that she drew blood, which she then coughed up, knowing that the Germans would see this as a sign of tuberculosis and run home, terrified. They freed her almost immediately.

BADASS RATING: ★★★★★
Britain's most daring special agent and Ian Fleming's inspiration for Vesper Lynd in his 007 novels.

MORE KICKASS Ks

KAMLA

Kamla Devi (b.1958) is a fifty-five-year-old widow who fought off a leopard with her own bare hands.

BADASS RATING: ★ ★ ★ ★ ★

KAREN

Karen Alexander, aka Kathy Acker (1944–97), buzz-cut sporting, tattooed novelist and feminist, performed in live sex shows with her boyfriend to fund her writing.

BADASS RATING: ★ ★ ★

KATHLEEN

Kathleen Hanna (b.1968) is a punk legend, feminist and founder of the riot grrrl movement.

BADASS RATING: ★ ★ ★ ★ ★

MORE KICKASS Ks

KEITH

Keith Richards (b.1943), founding member of the Rolling Stones, is the legend responsible for the greatest body of riffs on a guitar in rock history.

BADASS RATING: ★★★

KEN/KENULE

Ken Saro-Wiwa (1941–95) was the Nigerian environmental activist and author who took on the international petroleum industry to protect his homeland from oil drilling.

BADASS RATING: ★★★★★

KIA

Kia Silverbrook (b.1958), an Australian inventor with 9,874 patents to his name, is basically the most prolific inventor in the world.

BADASS RATING: ★★★

MORE KICKASS Ks

KOFI

Kofi Annan (1938–2018), former Secretary General of the United Nations, was a much-admired leader, man of peace and champion of human rights.

BADASS RATING: ★★★★

KŌSA

Kōsa (1543–92) was a Buddhist warrior who waged a ten-year war against the infamous Japanese ruler Nobunaga Oda.

BADASS RATING: ★★★

LASKARINA

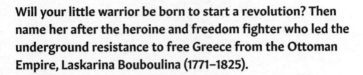

Will your little warrior be born to start a revolution? Then name her after the heroine and freedom fighter who led the underground resistance to free Greece from the Ottoman Empire, Laskarina Bouboulina (1771–1825).

When pirates killed her second husband, Laskarina was left with seven kids and a pretty sweet inheritance. Savvy, sassy and smart, she took over her husband's business, invested her money wisely and ended up with enough money to spend the rest of her days luxuriating in comfort. But of course, Laskarina was 100 per cent bona fide badass, and instead of kicking back she joined the *Filiki Etaireia* (Greek Society of Friends), built a warship named *Agamemnon* and began a rampage to overthrow Ottoman rule.

Throwing every penny of her estate into the war effort, Laskarina blazed across Mediterranean waters, commanding a fleet of six battleships. Along with her fellow revolters, she caused carnage among the Turks, eventually pushing them out of the city of Tripoli and making Greece independent.

BADASS RATING: ★★★★★
The heroine who put her ass and assets on the line to give Greece independence.

LAURENS

Will your little chap be full of cheek? Then name him after the mischievous marauder and French pirate captain, Laurens de Graaf (1653–1704).

Hailed as one of the hottest pirates to have ever ravaged the Caribbean, Laurens was known for having guns of steel, being insanely ripped and for playing sweet, sweet music to his crew. The man could command a violin like the lead of the Bergen Philharmonic and he wasn't bad at the trumpet either. Well read and with a penchant for Shakespeare, he could also recite *King Lear* by heart, which provided handy on-board entertainment during a long voyage.

Laurens came to his seafaring life as a law-abiding sailor, but later turned to privateering. He became so good at it that he successfully defeated pretty much any pirate fleet foolish enough to attack. When the Spaniards sent a full armada after him, he seized their squad and took the lead ship for his own. But being the gentleman that he was, rather than toss the injured Spanish captain overboard, he gave him a ride to the nearest piece of land to ensure that he would live.

BADASS RATING: ★★★★
The pirate with the full package, so to speak.

Leonid

Is the mini-dude kicking back in your womb giving you vibes of, 'Mama I'm so badass I'd whip out one of my organs with my own bare hands'? Yes? Then name him after Dr Leonid Ivanovich Rogozov (1934–2000). You'll soon see why.

While stationed in Antarctica, twenty-seven-year-old Leonid developed acute appendicitis. The only doctor for thousands of miles and stuck in a blizzard, Leonid swiftly realized that in order to give death the two fingers, he was going to have to submit to his own knife-wielding hands and operate on himself. With two of his crew standing by to pass tools, Leonid used just local anaesthetic, a couple of carefully placed mirrors and a scalpel to remove his appendix. All while running a raging fever, suffering nausea and all the other shit that goes with having a deadly infection.

Almost even more badass, he was back to work just two weeks later, like, 'Whatever, it was nothing, guys.'

BADASS RATING: ★★★★
Leonid blindly removed his own appendix in sub-zero temperatures.

LETITIA

Can you hear your little cherub's dulcet tones echoing up from your womb? Then name your babe after the woman who found her voice and changed the course of history, (Nellie) Letitia McClung (1873–1951).

A courageous warrior for equality, Letitia spent her life fighting to give women a place in society. She campaigned for mothers' allowances, birth control and free medical care, but the most defining victory in her crusade of badassery was when she changed Canadian law to legally acknowledge women as people.

Yep, you've read that right.

Up until 1929, women were not recognized persons in the law, and therefore could not sit in the Senate or do a bunch of other stuff, despite having the right to vote and, y'know, growing and birthing the whole population of Canada.

So Letitia made sure this was changed. She formed a kickass girl gang, known as the Famous Five, and together they rose up against the patriarchy. From the courts of Canada to the Houses of Parliament in London, Letitia's strength, power and persistence saw the law amended to include women as 'persons', which opened the doors of the Senate and paved the way for more equality.

BADASS RATING: ★ ★ ★ ★
The Canadian suffragette who shouted from the rooftops for change.

LILIAS

Is baby due on October 31st? Will this make her a fan of pointy hats and black cats, and make her willing to shack up with the devil? (Hey, as far as future boyfriends go, it could be worse...) Then why not make her the namesake of the rebel witch who took one for the team to save other women from a similar fate, Lilias Adie (d.1704).

Lilias was accused of witchcraft and sent to trial. She was brutally interrogated for sorcery, but refused to surrender the names of her sisters in a bid to save other women from wrongful convictions. Charged as the wife of the devil (seriously, how much whisky were the people of Scotland drinking back in 1704?), she was imprisoned, and condemned to be burnt at the stake. But being the bold and brazen badass that she was, she bravely drew her own noose instead, then proceeded to haunt the beaches of Fife for eternity.

BADASS RATING: ★★★★★
The babe with the power of voodoo who is forever immortalized in Scottish legend.

LILITH

Will your little maiden be strong, fearless and forthright? Then name her after Lilith (who lived a long, long time ago) – the woman who stormed out of the Garden of Eden after Adam denied her equality.

It is believed that Lilith was Adam's first wife, but her place in the Promised Land was revoked when she decided to give patriarchy a gentle punch to the face by (quite rightly) refusing to lie beneath him. Instead, she suggested that they lie together side by side, as equals. Of course, this went down like a lead balloon crashing out of the clouds of paradise, and Lilith was frog-marched out of Eden and subsequently demonized by history.

BADASS RATING: ★ ★ ★ ★ ★
The freakin' awesome goddess who basically got rejected from the Bible for daring to claim she was equal to a man. Attagirl!

LILIUOKALANI

Will your little princess be loyal and kind? Then name her after the first and last queen of Hawaii and totally rad royal, Liliuokalani (1838–1917).

As ruler of the kingdom of Hawaii, Liliuokalani was fiercely dedicated. She improved education, promoted the arts, set up trusts to help the orphaned and destitute, and worked tirelessly to protect the islands.

She was also the kind of badass queen who could just pick up a guitar or sit down casually at a piano or organ and belt out the sweetest musical delights. She composed over 160 songs, including the famous 'Aloha Oe', which Johnny Cash later covered.

With American businessmen hungry for Hawaii's sugar and pineapple plantations, Liliuokalani was eventually overthrown and imprisoned, but she didn't go down without the mother of all fights.

BADASS RATING: ★ ★ ★ ★
A queen who never stopped working for her people.

LILLIAN

Will you want to inspire your mini-me to soar to dizzying heights? Then name her after the queen of the air and star of the circus, Lillian Leitzel (1892–1931).

A captivating aerial gymnast, Lillian wowed audiences with her bold and daring routines. Suspended 15 metres above the ground, she would perform a sequence of the most outrageously difficult acrobatic moves with such skill and speed that spectators would leap into the air in awe. Her signature act was to turn her body into a human pinwheel and spin so rapidly that her shoulder would dislocate itself and then snap back with each turn – and she'd often perform over 200 of these spellbinding swingovers in one go.

BADASS RATING: ★★★★
An original diva and with skillz in abundance, Lillian became one of the most famous performers of the early twentieth century.

LORENZ

Want to encourage your son to go out and live his best life? Then name him Lorenz, after the awe-inspiring, wilderness-exploring Danish adventurer, Lorenz Peter Elfred Freuchen (1886–1957).

Some humans are just born epically cool. Lorenz was one of them. After studying to be a doctor, he decided it was time to ramp up the dial for adventure and set off on an expedition to the North Pole with one of his pals. He then lived there or thereabouts for the next fifteen years, marrying an Inuit and becoming fluent in Eskimo-Aleut as well as the language of badassitude.

He batted off frostbite, snow blindness, starvation and even being buried alive in a snowstorm, after which he spent thirty hours singlehandedly breaking out of his own icy tomb. From polar bear confrontations to amputating his own gangrenous toes to killing wolves with his bare hands, Lorenz's badassery knew no bounds.

But of course, it didn't end in the Arctic. When his wife died he returned to Denmark, bashed out thirty-odd books, wrote and starred as the villain in an Oscar-winning film and then became the fifth person to claim the jackpot of a TV show called *The $64,000 Question*. Phew.

BADASS RATING: ★ ★ ★ ★ ★
The explorer whose life of extreme adventure has made him a legend.

LOUISA

Are you growing a little iconoclast? Then name her after the radical writer who refused to conform, Louisa May Alcott (1832–88).

As a devout feminist who shirked marriage, Louisa despised the female fiction narrative of 'girl finds husband'. So when her publisher asked her to write a novel for women, she outright refused – 'Not on your nelly, mate.'

But with a dwindling bank balance and a persuasive publisher, she eventually succumbed, and knocked out *Little Women* in a mere ten weeks.

Given that Louisa was a headstrong, independent woman who shunned a life of subservience in favour of her career and ambitions, she had to create Jo March, a literary badass who simply refused to do what was expected of her. The novel Louisa didn't want to write was an instant bestseller and has become one of the most beloved stories of all time.

BADASS RATING: ★★★★
Author, empowering feminist, anti-slavery campaigner and rebel.

Lucille

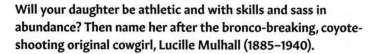

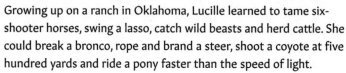

Will your daughter be athletic and with skills and sass in abundance? Then name her after the bronco-breaking, coyote-shooting original cowgirl, Lucille Mulhall (1885–1940).

Growing up on a ranch in Oklahoma, Lucille learned to tame six-shooter horses, swing a lasso, catch wild beasts and herd cattle. She could break a bronco, rope and brand a steer, shoot a coyote at five hundred yards and ride a pony faster than the speed of light.

In roping and riding competitions she owned it, winning first prize and making the other cowboys look like a bunch of sewn-up half-wit namby-pambies. She produced her own rodeo and toured the country, thrilling crowds with her daring acts. And when Teddy Roosevelt told her that if she could rope a wolf, he would invite her to some big-deal parade, she hollered at him, 'Alrighteee, y'loco son of a bitch!' and galloped up to him three hours later with a dead prairie wolf swinging behind her horse's legs.

BADASS RATING: ★★★★★
Gutsy, enchanting and with seriously mad skills.

Lucrezia

Can you feel a fire burning in your belly? Will your little diva be a bedazzling and beguiling badass? Then name her after the rebel daughter of a Renaissance pope, Lucrezia Borgia (1480–1519).

With an air of scandal already swirling, Lucrezia entered the world the illegitimate daughter of Alexander IV and his mistress. A legendary beauty, muse and patron of the arts, she was part of the infamous family known as the Borgias. She could also knock out any passing Italian dandy with a single punch.

The tattles told tales of Lucrezia carrying a phial of poison in a ring on her finger, should the need ever arise for it. It was believed that she attended wild orgies, often with up to a hundred eager participants slinking in to join the party.

History has tried to paint Lucrezia as an infamous murderess; whether or not there is any truth in the accusations, there's no denying that she was a fearless and formidable fireball who created a devilish legacy.

BADASS RATING: ★★
The riotous royal who didn't give a damn.

LYDIA

Will your daughter be born with extreme courage and an even stronger dose of badassery? Then name her after the gutsy and gallant flying ace who took the Nazis by their nuts and then swung them 360 degrees, Lydia Litvyak (1921–43).

Lydia began flying when she was fourteen. By fifteen, she was flying solo and was probably performing daily power dives, barrel rolls and high yoyos before she'd even had her morning coffee.

When the Soviet army starting recruiting women to help kick fascist ass mid-air, Lydia was already a flying instructor with forty-five trained-up pilots under her belt. It took her all of two combat missions to score her first solo aerial victory, becoming the first woman in history to kill an enemy mid-air. About ten seconds later she scored another victory, taking down an eleven-kill fighter ace and a recipient of the Iron Cross.

By 1943, she had twelve confirmed solo kills to her name, making her the highest-scoring female fighter ace in the world.

BADASS RATING: ★★★
One of the biggest daredevils to have ever entered a cockpit.

LYUDMILA

Perhaps your little firecracker will be born with a face that says, 'Mess with me and I will straight Fuck You Up'? In which case give her the name of the deadliest female sniper in the world, Lyudmila Pavlichenko (1916–74).

In June 1941, when Hitler invaded the Soviet Union, Lyudmila sacked off her university studies and stormed into the war effort as one of Russia's female snipers. In less than a year, a record 309 Nazis had fallen under her gun, 36 of them enemy snipers. Her hunts were dangerous and deadly. Some duels lasted for over three days; on other assignments, Lyudmila would endure twenty-hour stretches crouched in position, waiting for the perfect shot.

BADASS RATING: ★★★★
One of the most fearsome soldiers in military history, with a crack shot and hardcore ability to kick fascist ass.

MORE LUSTROUS Ls

LALLA

Lalla Fatma N'Soumer (1830–63) was the hard-as-nails Algerian freedom fighter who led a victory against a 13,000-strong French army.

BADASS RATING: ★★★★

LATIFAH

Queen Latifah (b.1970), bold, talented and a feminist pioneer, is the first hip-hop artist to have been nominated for an Oscar and has sold nearly two million records.

BADASS RATING: ★★★★

LAURENCE

Laurence Tureaud (b.1952), aka Mr. T, is the gold-chain-wearing hulk who went from burly bodyguard to taking Hollywood by storm as the hardman in *Rocky*.

BADASS RATING: ★★

MORE LUSTROUS Ls

LEONARDO

Leonardo Da Vinci (1452–1519) – awesome, ambidextrous inventor, scientist, artist and crazy person. Who else can say that one of their paintings was bought by the Louvre for a cool $650 million?

BADASS RATING: ★ ★ ★ ★

LIONEL

Lionel Wafer (1640–1705) shunned a career in the Welsh valleys for a rip-roaring adventure across the high seas as a pirate surgeon.

BADASS RATING: ★ ★ ★

LIVIA

Livia Drusilla (58 BC–29 AD), the wife of the first Roman emperor and illustrious mastermind behind Roman rule, is thought to have served as Emperor Augustus's political advisor and confidante.

BADASS RATING: ★ ★ ★

MORE LUSTROUS Ls

LOUIS

Louis Pasteur (1822–95) was the French chemist and microbiologist who saved a shitload of lives with his discoveries.

BADASS RATING: ★★★

LUCA

Luca Pacioli (*c.*1447–1517), an Italian mathematician who was Leonardo Da Vinci's housemate (and most likely beau), basically invented accounting.

BADASS RATING: ★★★

LUCAS

George Lucas (b.1944) – the dude who created *Star Wars*. Full stop. Tell that to your little stormtrooper when he asks why you gave him his name.

BADASS RATING: ★★★★

MORE LUSTROUS Ls

LUCY

Lucy Maud Montgomery (1874–1942) was the boundary-busting author who wrote *Anne of Green Gables* as well as another 20 novels, 530 short stories, 500 poems and a casual 30 essays. Attagirl!

BADASS RATING: ★★

LUIS

Luis Buñuel (1900–83) was the revolutionary Mexican filmmaker and pioneer of surrealist cinema who deliberately shocked, provoked and attacked bourgeois society.

BADASS RATING: ★★★★

LUTHER

Luther Blissett (b.1958) is the footballer who was signed by AC Milan for a cool $1,000,000 in 1983 – and has had his name nabbed by a bunch of activists, artists, poets and performers.

BADASS RATING: ★★★

MADGE

Will your babe twizzle and glide into the world? Then take inspiration from the triple-flipping, back-spinning, slide-chasséing ice queen who was the first woman to win Olympic gold in figure skating, Florence Madeline 'Madge' Syers (1881–1917).

A lean, mean, triple-axelling machine, Madge entered the 1902 World Championships, which up until that point only men had participated in. When officials realized that there was nothing in the rulebook that could explicitly exempt a woman, they reluctantly allowed her to compete. Of course, Madge won the silver medal. Down with the patriarchy!

Madge's next landmark victory was to storm the 1908 Olympics and take home gold, which she did by delivering one of figure skating's most difficult and death-defying jumps. She demonstrated the feat in a skirt shorter than the standard to show off her ankles – because she was a bodacious badass and that is how she rolled.

BADASS RATING: ★★★★
The brazen babe who dared to compete in an all-male competition, and changed the course of history.

MAI

Will your daughter be gutsy with guns of steel? Then name her after the elephant-riding, arrow-shooting bodyguard who led an army of Sikh soldiers to victory, Mai Bhago (b. *c.*1666).

Born in rural India, Mai was taught how to kick ass from an early age. From riding horses and elephants or blading anyone who looked menacing to defeating her enemies in hand-to-hand combat, it is fair to say that Mai was pretty hard, and you probably wouldn't want to mess with her.

Being Sikh, she lived under the control of a violent Mughal ruler, who saw her community as a rebel society and decided to launch an attack. One by one, Sikh soldiers were driven to a bloody end by the Mughal army, or escaped death's clutches by deserting their religion.

When Mai's own husband tried to pussyfoot out of the door, she took matters into her own hands. In 1705 she led forty soldiers back into battle against the invading Mughals and beat their brains out.

Prophet Guru Gobind Singh was so impressed with her badassery that he hired her as his bodyguard, after which she spent the rest of her days attacking anyone who got within two paces of him.

BADASS RATING: ★★★★
The Sikh warrior turned bodyguard who fought for freedom.

MALALA

Want to inspire your daughter to have courage in the face of adversity? Then name her after the teenager who fearlessly stood up for education, Malala Yousafzai (b.1997).

Malala was not afraid to fight for her right to education. At eleven years old, she captivated audiences with her blog for the BBC about her life under Taliban rule. She wrote under a pseudonym, but when her identity was revealed she became a target for the Taliban.

Malala was fifteen when she boarded a bus to school and was shot in the head and neck by a masked gunman. Her injuries were so severe that no one expected her to live, but Malala defiantly stared death in the face and refused to surrender. After weeks of intensive care, she survived. And since then she has become an icon of hope and courage, and an immensely powerful force for change.

The UN passed a petition in her name that led to the creation of Pakistan's very first Right to Education bill; Malala has launched an organization to help girls go to school worldwide, and has opened an all-girls school for Syrian refugees; oh, and she's also become the youngest person ever to be awarded a Nobel Peace Prize. A breathtaking inspiration.

BADASS RATING: ★★★★★
A total badass whose immense bravery inspired the world to act.

MALLOY

Growing a headstrong, stubborn little mule? Then name him after the invincible hardass and legend, Michael Malloy (1873–1933).

Malloy spent most of his life necking shots in some speakeasy on the upper side of New York, drifting in and out of casual employment and sleeping rough on the streets. All this made him an easy target for a couple of chancers keen on making some cash out of a sneaky life-insurance scam. Pinpointing Malloy as their route to riches, they decided to kill him. Only Malloy was made of extreme, hard-as-nails, hardcore, steely-balled, death-defying badassery with a side serving of being completely indestructible, and he relentlessly bounced back from their murderous attacks. He survived drinking antifreeze, eating rat poison, being thrown out and left for dead in −14 degree weather, being hit by a taxi at full throttle and various other acts of homicide. He was eventually knocked off, but became known as Iron Mike Malloy: the man it was impossible to kill.

BADASS RATING: ★★★
The guy who relentlessly gave death the finger.

MARGARET

Bamboozled by your new bae? Then name her after the boss who stuck two fingers up to the establishment, hole and corner, and, fooling the world into thinking she was a man, became a top surgeon – Margaret Bulkley (1795–1865).

Women had their place in nineteenth-century Ireland, but Margaret was having none of it. Determined to become a doctor, she reinvented herself as James Barry and scooted off to Edinburgh to study medicine. From the lecture halls of university to the gruelling regime of the British army, Margaret smashed military training and became one of the army's most renowned doctors.

All while masquerading as a man, Margaret was able to pioneer new techniques in medicine. She performed the first successful C-section in South Africa in 1826. Her skills and expertise led to her appointment as high society's most trusted private physician. She wasn't afraid to argue or show her eccentricities, never letting her guise slip; unbeknown to the blinded British Empire, Margaret was undeniably proving that women could achieve just as much, if not more, than men.

BADASS RATING: ★★★★★
The Irish visionary who rebelled against convention, duped the British elite and became the most celebrated surgeon of all time.

MARIE

Will your little tiger be curious about the world? Then name her after the trailblazing scientist whose medical breakthroughs continue to save countless lives today, Marie Curie (1867–1934).

From studying in an underground university in Warsaw to quench her thirst for knowledge to arriving in Paris to experiment in a makeshift shed that would eventually become her laboratory, Marie smashed gender barriers, pioneered scientific research and changed the world.

She was the first woman to win a Nobel Prize, which she took home in 1903 for her contribution to physics. But one Nobel Prize casually sitting on the mantelpiece wasn't enough; Marie made history again as the first person to be honoured with two chunky slabs of gold, winning her second Nobel Prize in 1911 in chemistry.

Alongside her husband, she discovered two new elements, radium and polonium, which she refused to patent because she was the kind of badass who had no desire to cash in on her genius. She developed the theory of radioactivity, set up field hospitals during the First World War, founded two medical research institutes in France and Poland and created an everlasting legacy.

BADASS RATING: ★ ★ ★ ★ ★
One of the greatest scientists and patriarchy-smashers of all time.

MARIYA

Growing a tour de force? Then name her after the woman who assembled a tank to wreak revenge on the Nazis for slaying her bae, Mariya Oktyabrskaya (1905–44).

When her husband was killed during the Second World War, Mariya sold everything she owned, deposited all her personal savings in the national bank and wrote a plea to Stalin that he allow her to build a tank, so that she could grenade the shit out of Hitler's army in retribution. Stalin said yes, and the avenging T-34 tank 'Fighting Girlfriend' was born. Mariya then surprised the Soviet army by effortlessly out-manoeuvring German soldiers with her tank, and then shelling them to smithereens. No sweat.

BADASS RATING: ★★★★
Don't mess with Mariya.

MARLON

Want to encourage your little one to stand up and fight for what is right? Then name him after the trailblazing African-American pilot who waged a war against discrimination, Marlon DeWitt Green (1929–2009).

When Marlon applied for a job as a pilot with Continental Airlines, he didn't bother to submit a photo with his application. He took the entrance exam, passed with flying colours, and then was rejected for the role.

Marlon had over nine years of experience flying in the US air force; he could perform 360-degree loops and barrel rolls in his sleep, navigate bombers at full throttle, glide rescue planes and basically make anything with an engine soar across the sky.

The five other white applicants who had far less experience were hired. So in 1963, Marlon took on Continental Airlines, sued their asses for racial discrimination, and won. The ruling was a landmark victory in America and opened the door for hundreds of other minority pilots.

BADASS RATING: ★★★★
The guy who smashed his way through the colour barrier to become the first African-American commercial airline pilot.

MARY

Want to feed your daughter's curiosity? Then name her after the nineteenth-century fossil-hunter, Mary Anning (1799–1847).

It was pretty obvious that Mary was destined for greatness when she was struck by lightning as a babe in arms, and survived. The fire bolt instantly killed the three women holding her, so when Mary was found alive, it was declared a miracle.

In Lyme Regis, England, as her family had little money, Mary and her siblings learned to collect shells on their local beach, selling them to make ends meet. From trading fossils on the seashore, Mary turned into a fossil-hunter extraordinaire, unearthing prehistoric gems from wild, weather-ravaged cliffs with amazing skill. She dug up the skeletons of prehistoric sea creatures, painstakingly extracted dinosaur fossils from 205-million-year-old cliffs and uncovered the skeleton of a pterosaur – a flying dinosaur not previously found in Britain. She also identified fossilized dinosaur shit. #lifegoals

Mary's groundbreaking discoveries delivered new insights into the history of the earth and paved the way for future scientific breakthroughs.

BADASS RATING: ★★★★
The unofficial palaeontologist who made some of the most significant geological finds of all time.

MASHA

Will your little rebel rise up and start a revolution? Then name her after the punk-feminist protester and founder of Pussy Riot, Maria 'Masha' Alyokhina (b.1988).

On 21 February 2012, Masha and the other four members of the punk collective Pussy Riot stormed the main cathedral in Moscow, taking to the altar for a righteous performance of their very own punk prayer, 'Virgin Mary, drive out Putin!' Clad in fluorescent balaclavas and bright hosiery, Masha and her sisters performed this legendary protest for an epic forty seconds before being ambushed by security.

BADASS RATING: ★★★★
A brazen, bold and brave badass who has become an international symbol of radical resistance.

MATA

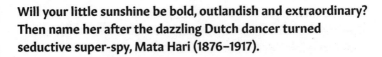

Will your little sunshine be bold, outlandish and extraordinary? Then name her after the dazzling Dutch dancer turned seductive super-spy, Mata Hari (1876–1917).

The original femme fatale and with more sass than you could shake a sass stick at, Mata's life was a whirlwind of wild adventures. At eighteen she answered a lonely hearts ad by a Dutch captain seeking a wife, married him in a fluorescent yellow gown and sailed off to live a romantic life on an island in the West Indies. When her husband became abusive, she fled to Paris, arriving penniless. She then reinvented herself as the world's most famous exotic dancer, pretended she was raised in the jungle and delighted audiences with a striptease that involved a silk scarf and a bejewelled intimate area.

From wowing Parisian theatres, Mata moved on to serving as a daring spy in the First World War; she had many lovers and wove a web of many lies. As war paranoia set in, the French became suspicious, and accused her of being a double agent. Mata denied the charges, but for the first and only time in her life, her fate lay in someone else's hands.

BADASS RATING: ★★★★
The mysterious and magnetic dancer who became the First World War's most famous spy.

LA MAUPIN

Will your little rascal be born free spirited? Then name her after the free-loving, cross-dressing French opera singer and swordswoman, La Maupin (1670–1707).

A rebellious young La Maupin succeeded in an ultimate teenage act of parental defiance by banging her dad's boss. So when the most mediocre of all men in Marseille rolled into her village, La Maupin was married off quicker than you can say Jack Robinson. But this babe was not about to be tied down to a tame life as the wife of a taxman. Instead she took off with a renowned swordsman who taught her the art of fencing, and together they toured across France performing duels.

La Maupin was a master fighter and would notoriously begin each duel with a song. She was also insanely promiscuous, and anyone who gave her any beef for it quickly met the end of her sword. After a brief stint in a convent, where she took holy orders to continue an illicit affair with a nun, La Maupin wound up in Paris, landed the lead role in a highly esteemed opera and famously continued to bonk and brawl her way across town.

BADASS RATING: ★★
From street fighter to opera star, La Maupin was a sensational hellraiser.

MAXWELL

Will your future son be a free spirit with deadly charisma? Then name him after the American poet, novelist and bohemian, Maxwell Bodenheim (1892–1954).

After knocking out more than a few well-received novels and poetry books, Maxwell decided to take the whole tortured artist gig to another level. He dropped out of society, embraced the life of a hobo and wandered the streets of New York with his wife in tow – and a brown paper bag concealing eight cans of the 1930s equivalent of Special Brew.

When he needed more supplies, he would simply rock up to one of the literati's parties with an empty bag and fill his boots with anything left on the tables. On one occasion Maxwell turned up at screenwriter Ben Hecht's house, and while other guests enjoyed French 75s on the roof, Maxwell ransacked Ben's closet. He took off with his socks, shorts, ties, shirts, pyjamas and a pair of new shoes – more than enough to kick-start his park bench autumn/winter capsule wardrobe for that year.

Prior to his days as a loaded drifter, Maxwell was quite the lady-killer – in every sense of the term. In a string of unfortunate events, three of his ex-lovers committed suicide and another was killed by a subway train. It is no surprise that after that, few women in town went near his crown jewels again.

BADASS RATING: ★★
The king of bohemia.

MAY

Will your daughter dazzle the world with her daring acts? Then name her after the somersaulting queen of the circus who performed the most insane stunts on horseback, May Wirth (1894–1978).

May grew up in the circus, toddling across high wires when most kids had only just mastered crawling, and practising contortion before she could write her own name. May was able, athletic and completely ready to be awesome.

From hopping on a horse aged ten to becoming the world's greatest bareback rider, May's famous act combined acrobatics and horseriding with some death-defying wizardry thrown in for fun. She would leap blindfolded from the ground onto the back of a galloping stallion. She would then proceed to somersault in the air between running ponies, landing gracefully on the back of each animal before launching herself into the sky again. With swarms of admirers across the globe flocking to see her sensational act, she was one of the most famous circus performers in history.

BADASS RATING: ★★★★
Took sass and stunt-riding to another level.

MAYA

Want to inspire your daughter to go out into the world and kick ass? Then name her after all-round badass babe, the American poet and civil rights activist, Maya Angelou (1928–2014).

Maya smashed through every racial and gender barrier in America to completely own it as a writer, activist and rad human being.

She flipped the bird to the obscene laws in place that forbade interracial marriage, and married for love. She studied dance, performed across Europe and starred in the opera before stealing hearts as a writer. She knocked out an impressive thirty-six books including fiction, non-fiction and poetry. Her debut novel, *I Know Why the Caged Bird Sings*, wasn't afraid to deal with the issues of rape, racism and drug abuse, which led to it becoming one of the most banned books in America.

Maya was the first African-American woman to write a screenplay that was made into a film. She was the first female poet to write and perform at a presidential inauguration. She won a bunch of badass awards for her immense talents, including a Pulitzer Prize, an Emmy and three Grammys for her spoken word albums; then in 2010 she took home the highest honour possible in the United States – the Presidential Medal of Freedom.

Badass quote: 'Life's a bitch. You've got to go out and kick ass.'

BADASS RATING: ★★★★★
A littérateur legend who possessed awesomeness in abundance.

MELITTA

Bubba born to soar the skies? Take inspiration from Melitta von Stauffenberg (1903–45).

Aeronautical engineer, test pilot and second ever woman to qualify as an aircraft captain, razor-sharp Melitta did test dives fifteen times a day from heights of 4,000 metres (13,000 ft) throughout the Second World War. She was also the brains behind revolutionary blind flying instruments and systems that enabled Luftwaffe fighters to intercept night-time enemy bombers. But while the Führer might have thought of her as his secret weapon, she stuck fiercely to her principles and supported the famous attempt to assassinate him.

BADASS RATING: ★★★
Whip-smart, fearless, a chick who went down in aviation history.

MHAIRI

Will your wee one be kind, caring and a total trailblazer for a new generation? Then name her after the banging, no-nonsense Scottish MP and woman of the people, Mhairi Black (b.1994).

In 2015 Mhairi became the youngest person ever to be elected into the Houses of Parliament, winning her seat at the age of twenty. Her maiden speech kicked so much ass it had ten million online views within a few days, and was even trending in Nigeria. Since then Mhairi has relentlessly called out MPs who have 'talked shite' and told lies. A powerhouse on a mission to make parliament better represent its people, Mhairi has never hidden her disdain for Westminster or the fact that she reckons it might be full of sociopaths – some of whom she might like to put on the receiving end of a much-deserved Glaswegian kiss.

BADASS RATING: ★★★★
Principled, passionate and a total badass.

MICHAEL

Want to encourage your little sport never to give up in the pursuit of his dreams? Then name him after the unlikely British ski jumper turned Olympic legend, Michael Edwards, aka Eddie the Eagle (b.1963).

At the start of 1988, Michael was a casual plasterer from the West Country with big ambitions. By February he had taken the world by storm as the British ski jump entry at the Winter Olympics in Calgary, Canada. Due to a technical loophole in the ski jump competition rules, he was able to breeze in as Team Great Britain's entry, despite not really having the necessary athletic qualifications.

Michael's training had been entirely self-funded and consisted of travelling across Europe in his mum's wheels, borrowing skis from Austrians, a helmet from a generous Italian and attempting his very first jump with the grit and determination of a pure legend.

Michael may have been slightly overweight, extremely short-sighted and a man of mediocre athletic ability, but that did not stop him chasing his Olympic dreams. When his jaw broke during training, he tied it up with an old pillowcase. When his funds ran out, he took part-time jobs. This guy thought nothing of throwing himself off a 90-metre jump, kamikaze-style, to follow his heart.

And when the tournament rolled round, Michael may have come last in every single competition, but he miraculously managed to avoid both death and paralysis to become an international hero.

BADASS RATING: ★★★★★
The underdog who proved that what he lacked in skill, he made up for in BADASSITUDE.

MILDRED

Will your little bebe be born with epic athletic prowess? Then name her after one of the greatest sportswomen in history, Mildred 'Babe' Didrikson Zaharias (1911–56).

Mildred stormed into the sporting limelight in 1932 when she competed in US women's track and field championships as the entire team representing an insurance company. While her competitors turned up with at least a bus full of athletes, Mildred hopped onto the track and singlehandedly competed in all eight events. From the hurdles to the high jump, the shot put and the discus throw, she raced between starting lines, scooping first place in five of the eight competitions and going on to win the championship. In case that hasn't sunk in... Mildred won the entire competition, all by herself.

Following her roaring entrance into the sporting arena, she took it up a level in the 1932 Olympics. Of the three races she was allowed to enter, she took home gold in two of them – the javelin and 80m hurdles. She won a silver for the high jump, which would have been gold were it not for a minor technicality on one of her jumps that nowadays wouldn't matter; and she set world records in every event in which she competed.

Now queen of the track, field and basketball court, she decided to take up golf, and made history by entering the all-male Los Angeles Open. She went on to win fourteen golf tournaments in a row.

BADASS RATING: ★★★★★
A woman who owned it in every sporting field.

MILLICENT

Want to encourage your daughter to stand up and speak out for what she believes? Then name her after the courageous suffragette, Millicent Fawcett (1847–1929).

Millicent was nineteen when she steam-rolled into parliament, delivering a petition calling for women to have the vote. By the age of twenty-two, she was becoming a well-known speaker, inspiring others to join the suffrage movement and championing education for all. She founded Newnham College, Cambridge in 1871, opening the doors of academia for women. Known for her grace, poise, flame-red hair and killer speeches, she was elected president of the National Union of Women's Suffrage Societies in 1897, and helped the party gain over 100,000 members by 1913.

Preferring peaceful protest, Millicent was an instrumental leader in the campaign for women's right to vote. Badass.

BADASS RATING: ★★★★★
A legendary political activist who waged war against the patriarchy to win women the right to vote.

MUHAMMAD

Want to make your son the namesake of the biggest boxing legend in history? Call him after the guy who floated like a butterfly but stung like a bee, Muhammad Ali (1942–2016).

Three-time world heavyweight champion, Olympic gold medallist and ardent civil rights activist, Muhammad was one of the greatest humans to grace the earth with his epically cool presence. Before a boxing match began, he would perform his own poetry, predicting the round in which he would knock out his opponent, and then step into the ring and deliver his prophecies.

Witty, wise and an outrageous showman who could throw a punch at a speed of 700 mph,* Muhammad was immensely courageous both inside and outside the ring. He wasn't afraid to stand up for his beliefs or call out racism, sexism and fascism. An anti-war campaigner, his refusal to support the Vietnam War led to him being stripped of his championship titles, passport and boxing licences and sentenced to five years in jail. Eventually pardoned, Muhammad continued to astonish the world with his awe-inspiring badassery until he passed away in 2016.

* This might be an exaggeration.

BADASS RATING: ★★★★★
Principled, passionate, poetic and one of THE greatest fighters in the world.

Muriel

Will your demoiselle be daring, determined and willing to go to great heights to change the world? Then name her after the bold and brave suffragette and journalist, Muriel Lilah Matters (1877–1969).

On 28 October 1908, Muriel shackled herself to the iron grille – a metal screen that obscures women's view of parliamentary debates – in the Ladies' Gallery in the House of Commons. It was a famously symbolic moment in the fight for suffrage, and the words she spoke that day are marked as the first to be delivered by a woman in the House.

From inside parliament to the clouds above: Muriel made headlines once more when she soared across London in a dirigible balloon, illuminating the sky with 'VOTES FOR WOMEN' emblazoned in enormous letters on the side of the airship and raining 25 kilos (56 lb) of Women's Freedom League pamphlets onto the streets of London.

She toured the country in a caravan, empowering thousands of women to join the cause; she stood as the Labour candidate in the 1924 general election, paving the way for women to enter Westminster, and tirelessly campaigned for social change.

BADASS RATING: ★★★★★
The damsel who pulled down the patriarchy.

MORE MARVELLOUS Ms

MAE

Mae Jemison (b.1956), the dancer, doctor and astronaut who became the first African-American woman in space, zoomed into orbit as the mission specialist on the *Endeavor* in September 1992. Mae also appeared in *Star Trek: The Next Generation* – the first ever real-life astronaut to grace the cult series. A badass who boldly went where no badass had gone before.

BADASS RATING: ★★★★

MAGNUS

Magnus Heinason (1548–89) was a swashbuckling buccaneer who sank any Englishman brave enough to cross into Norwegian waters.

BADASS RATING: ★★

MARIUCCIA

Mariuccia Mandelli (1925–2015) was a maverick Italian fashion designer who shook up the fashion world and invented the hot pant.

BADASS RATING: ★★★

MORE MARVELLOUS Ms

MARLOWE

Christopher Marlowe (1564–93), Renaissance poet, playwright and spy, foiled an assassination plot on Queen Elizabeth and caused a scandal with his alleged atheism and subsequently dramatic death.

BADASS RATING: ★★★

MARSHA

Marsha P. Johnson (1945–92) was a charming revolutionary African-American trans-activist and queen who pioneered the gay liberation movement in the United States.

BADASS RATING: ★★★★

MARTHA

Martha Graham (1894–1991), one of the most influential choreographers of the twentieth century, was the first dancer to perform at the White House.

BADASS RATING: ★★

MORE MARVELLOUS Ms

MARTY

Marty Stuart (b.1958) was a country music pioneer and king of the honky tonk.

BADASS RATING: ★★

MATILDA

Matilda of Canossa (1046–1115), one of the most powerful women of the Middle Ages, ruled Italy, pretty much acted as the pope's own personal bodyguard and won every military battle in her life.

BADASS RATING: ★★★★

MAUD

Maud Hunt (1873–1954) was an outrageous American painter and printmaker, who shunned convention, shacked up with an equally flamboyant female and blazed a trail of badassery across the art world.

BADASS RATING: ★★

MORE MARVELLOUS Ms

MAXIMILIAN

Maximilian Kolbe (1894–1941), a Polish priest with extraordinary courage, sacrificed his own life in Auschwitz in order to save a man with two children.

BADASS RATING: ★★★★★

MINNIE

Minnie Feodorovna (1847–1928) was a rebel princess who saved a man's life with a sneaky punctuation mark*.

BADASS RATING: ★★

*Minnie's husband, Tsar Alexander III of Russia, had signed an order that would knock off an alleged traitor. Scrawled next to the man's name was 'Pardon impossible, to be sent to Siberia'. Minnie casually rubbed out the comma and reinserted it to read 'Pardon, impossible to be sent to Siberia' so that the accused could walk free.

MIRIAM

Miriam Makeba (1932–2008) was a Grammy-winning South African singer and political activist.

BADASS RATING: ★★★★

MORE MARVELLOUS Ms

MISTY

Misty Copeland (b.1982) was the first African-American woman to be named a principal dancer in the seventy-five-year history of American ballet.

BADASS RATING: ★★★

MIYAMOTO

Miyamoto Musashi (1584–1645) was an invincible Japanese duel-sword fighting samurai who won every combat in his life, including destroying a force sent to ambush him with his epic swordsman skills.

BADASS RATING: ★★★★

NANA

Will your future daughter love to learn? Then name her after the Nigerian princess, poet and education pioneer, Nana Asma'u (1793–1864).

Nana was smart. In childhood she learned all the Islamic classics and mastered four languages, and by the age of fifteen she was advising army generals on their war tactics: legend has it that her casual suggestion to burn a battlefield in Alkalawa helped win a famous war in Nigeria.

Nana also practised poetry with swagger. She wrote about the divine truth, female warriors, saints and the rights of women. She wrote about culture and the turbulent politics of her time. But it was not just her poetry that created her legacy.

In a bid to smash the patriarchy and empower her fellow sisters, Nana made up an entire educational system. Called the *'yan taru*, it worked like an underground knowledge factory taught entirely in the form of the spoken word, and that anyone could learn. Nana assembled an all-girl gang of teachers and they journeyed across the country to pass on the wisdom to other women. It was so accessible, women could learn while doing their domestic work and without needing the approval of their husbands. What started in Nigeria spread across the globe; much of Nana's genius system is still in existence in parts of the world today.

BADASS RATING: ★★★★★
The lyricist who liberated women by finding a way to help them learn.

NANCY

Will your future daughter be glamorous, gutsy and fizzing with fortitude? Then name her after the daring British agent and most decorated servicewoman of the Second World War, Nancy Grace Augusta Wake (1913–2011).

When New Zealand-born Nancy inherited a few bob from her late aunt, she hot-footed it across the Pacific, landing in New York and then London, before shacking up with a Frenchman and moving to Marseille to quaff Cheval Blanc and smoke Gauloises in abundance. When the Second World War broke out, she joined the French Resistance. Nicknamed 'The White Mouse' by the Nazis for her fabulous ability to evade their capture, Nancy was top of the Führer's most wanted list with a five million-franc warrant to her name. The Gestapo tapped her telephone and intercepted her mail; but Nancy made sure she was never caught.

In 1942 she headed to Britain where she was trained in combat, became a dab hand at night parachuting and generally starred as one of their most celebrated special agents.

Nancy thought nothing of judo-chopping SS guards, pedalling over 500 kilometres on a pushbike across enemy camps or parachuting into danger zones. She is credited with helping hundreds of Allied soldiers escape Nazi persecution; she fought the Germans by any means she could, and is forever remembered as one of the greatest and sassiest secret agents of all time.

BADASS RATING: ★★★★★
The spunky spy who took on the most challenging of missions with the nonchalance of a Siamese cat.

Napoleon

Will your future son be formidable, fearless and a total hardass? Then name him after the army general turned self-appointed French ruler who thought nothing of waging war against every single power in Europe: Napoleon Bonaparte (1769–1821).

Born on a small island in the Mediterranean to a distinctly average family of very minor nobility, Napoleon rose to become emperor of France, king of Italy (briefly) and one of the greatest political and military rebels of all time.

An overachieving child prodigy with more political prowess than the love child of Julius Caesar and Alexander the Great, Napoleon was fighting to free his birthplace, Corsica, from French rule before he was old enough to even attend school. At nine years old he moved to mainland France, where he could have a better crack at world domination. He joined the French army, was rapidly promoted to commander, and his first taste of influence was coercing Austria and its allies to make peace. He then conquered Ottoman-ruled Egypt, attempted to block all British trade routes with India before staging a *coup d'état* and crowning himself emperor of France.

From centralizing the government and creating the first bank to fighting for the emancipation of European Jews, Napoleon managed to both promote religious tolerance and peace while attempting to destroy every single major power in Europe in a series of attacks known as the Napoleonic Wars.

BADASS RATING: ★★★★
A military maestro who would have had Beethoven's third symphony dedicated to him, if only he hadn't cocked up the Battle of Waterloo.

NATHANIEL

Will your future son have an uncanny ability to swim long distances in shark-infested waters? Then name him after one of the greatest sea-rovers in the Golden Age of piracy, Nathaniel North (1671–c.1707).

If there could be an award for 'best supporting buccaneer' in the world of piracy, then Nathaniel North would win hands down. Most of his pillaging life was spent sailing the high seas as the esteemed wingman to various pirate captains of high regard. Never one to miss some loot, Nathaniel once hijacked an eighteen-gun ship along the coast of Madagascar before speeding across the sea, attacking British, Danish and Indian crews with more velocity than a peregrine falcon mid-flight.

Nathaniel was known for his sly escapes. One time he evaded the Royal Navy by throwing himself overboard, faking his own drowning in an Oscar-worthy performance and then clandestinely swimming some 48 kilometres to shore. Another time, a brutal storm flipped his boat upside down, disseminating seamen across the west coast of America; but Nathaniel once again fought against the currents to swim an insane distance to dry land.

BADASS RATING: ★★★
A brutal buccaneer with mind-blowing swagger.

NELLIE

Want your daughter to feel like she can do anything? Then name her after the woman who invented undercover journalism and then used it to change the world, Nellie Bly (1864–1922).

When a newspaper took sexism to another level in a column called 'What Girls Are Good For', Nellie called them out in a stern letter to the editor. Her complaint was so eloquent that she was immediately offered the position of staff writer. She accepted the job and, in a bid to dispel the idea that female journalists were only good enough to write 'ladies' sections' in newspapers, Nellie took her reporting up a notch, refused to shy away from tackling hard-hitting issues and swiftly moved from writing for local rags to making the headlines in New York nationals.

When asked to put together a short piece on 'New York nut houses', Nellie decided the only way to discover what these institutions were really like was to feign insanity and get committed. During her ten days of incarceration, Nellie witnessed inhuman, shocking and scandalous practices, which she wrote an exposé on and used her experience to launch a campaign for reform. As a result of Nellie's eye-opening investigation, the City of New York then spent over $1,000,000 on improving its care for the mentally ill.

Nellie also uncovered the cruel conditions of sweatshop workers, called out corruption in the Mexican government (and got booted out of the country for doing so) and famously travelled solo around the world in seventy-two days, covering over 40,000 kilometres (25,000 miles) and writing an account of her voyage for the *New York World*. What a badass.

BADASS RATING: ★★★★
A daring pioneer of investigative journalism who risked her life to uncover some of the greatest scandals of her time.

NETTIE

Want to inspire your daughter to create and follow her own path? Then name her after the pioneering American geneticist, Nettie Maria Stevens (1861–1912).

Back in the nineteenth century, women were expected to pursue a life of dependent domestic drudgery and people believed things like having sex under a full moon meant any baby conceived would be a girl. Enter Nettie – hardworking, determined and ready to make history. She brushed off the notion that women were inferior, soaked up every ounce of education she was offered and in between teaching, studying and saving for further training, she made a discovery that would change genetics forever.

While examining butterflies and beetle larvae, Nettie found that male sperm carried both X and Y chromosomes, whereas female eggs carried just the X chromosome. From this she was able to prove that the sex of an unborn child comes from the sperm, not environmental factors, as previously believed. In 1905 Nettie published her paper *Studies in Spermatogenesis*, one of the greatest contributions to the field of genetics to this day.

BADASS RATING: ★★★★★
Smart AF ground-breaking scientist and all-round badass.

NICHOLAS

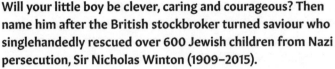

Will your little boy be clever, caring and courageous? Then name him after the British stockbroker turned saviour who singlehandedly rescued over 600 Jewish children from Nazi persecution, Sir Nicholas Winton (1909–2015).

A few months before the outbreak of the Second World War, Nicholas was about to hit the Swiss slopes for his annual skiing holiday when he received a call from his friend in Prague, a city hiding thousands of Jewish refugees fleeing the Nazis. Nicholas immediately threw down his ski boots and journeyed over to Czechoslovakia, determined to help. He wandered the streets of Prague, noting the refugee children's names and addresses; he took photographs and established a committee headquarters from his hotel room. After three weeks of annual leave, Nicolas was forced to return to work and flew back to London. Armed with a long list of children who needed rescuing, he spent his evenings and weekends blazing through the bureaucratic nightmare that is smuggling over 600 refugees – forging entry permits and scouting out placements and families to home each child. Within a few months, he had set up the transportation and documents needed to bring the children over to the UK.

That summer, Nicolas saved 660 children before casually resuming his daily business like it was absolutely nothing. Some fifty years later, when his heroism was made public in England, he was knighted for his mission; yet he remained humbly modest about what he had achieved.

BADASS RATING: ★★★★★
The sleuth hero who saved hundreds of lives.

NIKOLA

Will your little spark light up the world with his inventions? Then name him after the great visionary whose ground-breaking work gave the world electricity straight out of a socket, Nikola Tesla (1856–1943).

Pal of Mark Twain, rocker of an almighty moustache and architect of brilliance, Nikola was a prolific inventor with over 700 patents to his name. But his legacy lies in the mind-blowing accomplishments he made in the fields of magnetism and electricity, many of which paved the way for modern electrical transmissions, solar energy systems and smartphone technology.

Born in Serbia during a lightning storm, Nikola was an electric eccentric who liked to communicate with pigeons and was a staunch champion of the number three, as well as a genius. While walking in a Budapest park reciting poetry with a dear friend one day, he suddenly had a flash of inspiration that fired his idea for the development of alternating electrical current. Legend has it that he sketched out his ideas in the sand to his patient (and no doubt slightly bewildered) friend.

A total dynamo, Nikola went on to pioneer the fluorescent light, laser beams, wireless communications, remote control, robotics, vertical aircraft take-off and many other insanely awesome inventions.

BADASS RATING: ★★★★
Hailed as the father of physics and one of the twentieth century's greatest inventors, Nikola gave us the power.

NINA

Can you hear sweet, dulcet tones echoing out from your pregnant belly? Then name your little songstress after one of the greatest singers and activists of the twentieth century, Nina Simone (born Eunice Kathleen Waymon, 1933–2003).

Nina was a musical prodigy who refused to be pigeonholed. Known across her hometown for her insane piano-playing skills, Nina dreamed of becoming the first black concert pianist to play at Carnegie Hall. She won a scholarship to music college, playing in bars to pay the bills. When a bar owner suggested one evening that she stand up and sing, it sparked the beginning of her career as one of America's most awe-inspiring vocalists.

Nina battled oppression on every level; she shunned the greed of others and went on to produce over forty bestselling albums. She wrote anthems for the American civil rights movement, including 'Mississippi Goddam' after the 1963 Birmingham church bombing, and used music to make a stand against racism, sexism and bigotry. This high priestess of soul and her mind-blowing talent have left a lasting legacy in every corner of the world.

BADASS RATING: ★ ★ ★ ★ ★
A fearless protest artist, lyrical legend and civil rights activist – 100 per cent bona fide badass.

NOOR

Will your daughter be gutsy and gallant? Then name her after the Indian princess turned daring secret agent, Noor Inayat Khan (1914–44).

In 1943, Noor parachuted down into enemy-occupied France. She had recently joined the British spy network as the Special Operations Executive's first female radio operator, and Paris was her first assignment. Her mission was deemed so dangerous that Noor had been given a life expectancy of just six weeks.

In her first week, she watched almost the entire Parisian spy network go under. Outsmarting and then outrunning the Gestapo, Noor was left as the sole radio operator in the city. She then spent the next few months playing an increasingly menacing game of cat and mouse. She dodged Nazis, kicked de Fuhrer's ass and did the work of about twenty people to ensure that vital war information made it back to Churchill's HQ.

After four months of evading capture, Noor was betrayed by a double agent and arrested. Chained, placed in solitary confinement and put on a gourmet diet of potato scraps, she was tortured and interrogated, but Noor refused to surrender even an ounce of information. Ten months later she was shot. Her parting word was '*Liberté*'.

BADASS RATING: ★★★★★
Hero, total badass and queen.

NORA

Will your little possum be waggish, wry and writerly? Want to encourage her to find her own distinct voice? Then name her after the queen of the zinger who went from ink-slinger to trailblazing screenwriter and director, Nora Ephron (1941–2012).

It is thanks to Nora's courage to create bold, headstrong characters that films like *When Harry Met Sally*, *Sleepless in Seattle* and *You've Got Mail* led a movement in Hollywood. Her work encouraged others to produce films about smart, sassy and independent women. Creator of that legendary restaurant scene with the fake orgasm, Nora smashed the glass ceiling of Hollywood with her frank and fearless female leads, becoming not only one of the first female screenwriters in Tinseltown but a pioneering female director too.

From humble beginnings as a White House intern (where she claimed to be the only employee JFK didn't try to sleep with), Nora moved through manning the post room of *Newsweek* to filling the column inches of the *New York Post* and *Esquire* with frank, straight-talking writing rich in wit and style. Nora wasn't afraid to talk about sex, breasts or her love of food. She was champion of female empowerment and an ardent feminist. In her lifetime, Nora knocked out fourteen screenplays and smashed the box office countless times; she wrote eight books and three plays, and received several Oscar nominations and half a dozen awards for her contribution to the film industry.

BADASS RATING: ★★★★
Wisecracking leader who conquered Hollywood, tore apart gender stereotypes and inspired a new generation of female comics.

NORMA

Want to inspire your future daughter to live out her dreams through hard work, determination and a dose of badassery? Then name her after the Oscar-winning American actor who defied her critics, Norma Shearer (1902–83).

Ambitious and armed only with courage, Norma burst onto the scene in New York to audition for Broadway. But the chauvinist running the show declared her a 'dog' and told her she was 'too short', 'too chunky' and 'too cross-eyed' to ever become a showgirl. Penniless, squashed into small, dank digs with her mother and sister and in desperate need of income, Norma refused to give up her dream of acting. Instead she charmed her way into Universal Pictures to land a role as an extra, and worked tirelessly. When that job dried up, she posed with laundry soap, modelled dental floss, cheap tyres – anything and everything – before eventually she landed her break in film, starring in a B movie.

Norma's perseverance paid off. From living down and out in New York she moved to the hills of Hollywood, and went on to have one of the most successful film careers of the 1930s. She shunned conventional roles to play spunky, sexually liberated women, rightfully earning an Oscar for her leading role in *The Divorcee* and a place on the Hollywood Walk of Fame.

BADASS RATING: ★ ★ ★ ★
A smart, sassy and gutsy siren of the screen.

MORE NASTY/NOBLE Ns

NANAK

Guru Nanak (1469–1539) was the spiritual sage, religious rebel and innovator who founded the Sikh religion.

BADASS RATING: ★★★★★

NED

Ned Ludd (1700s–1800s) was the badass leader of the Luddites, a rebel gang of British textile workers who fought back against the rise of machines over manual labour.

BADASS RATING: ★★★★

NNIMMO

Nnimmo Bassey (b.1958) is a Nigerian environmentalist activist, architect and poet on an awe-inspiring crusade to clean up the terrors caused by the oil industry.

BADASS RATING: ★★★★

MORE NASTY/NOBLE Ns

NWANYERUWA

Nwanyeruwa (b.*c*.1900) was the Nigerian rebel who led a peaceful protest that has since become known as the Women's War – the first major revolt against West African colonizers.

BADASS RATING: ★★★★

NZINGA

Nzinga Mbande (1583–1663), queen of Angola and Portuguese freedom fighter, became famous for attacking oppressive systems and for her brutal and effective military tactics; legend has it she drank more human blood than Dracula.

BADASS RATING: ★★★

OCTAVIA

Will your daughter be brave, bold and brilliant? Then name her after the strident feminist, purveyor of the extraordinary and grand dame of science fiction, Octavia Estelle Butler (1947–2006).

From the towering teenage rebel who spent her days camped out in the Pasadena public library devouring novels, defying her then-undiagnosed dyslexia and writing stories in a giant pink notebook, Octavia moved on to author eighteen novels and short story collections and win over a dozen awards for her outstanding work.

Octavia created bestsellers; she wrote without borders and refused to be caged by race, class and gender. She took odd temping jobs (she once worked as a potato chip inspector #respect) so she could rise each morning at 2 a.m. and put all her energy into writing. She gave us stories of male pregnancy, aliens, time travel and vampires, all with terrifying insights into society at the time. Octavia stepped into a world that was predominately white and male and she shook it up like a totally trailblazing badass, whom we shall forever admire.

BADASS RATING: ★ ★ ★ ★
A genius who made her own world and changed the landscape of science fiction.

Odette

Will the little astronaut floating in your utero be dauntless, determined and with more dare than a Versace dress held together by only a couple of safety pins*? Then name her after the spunky Second World War British spy, Odette Hallowes (1912–95).

Odette swanned into her role in the Special Operations Executive by complete accident. On hearing a radio advert seeking holiday photos of French beaches to help prepare raids for the reinvasion of Europe, Odette sent some snaps, along with a letter explaining she was born in France and knew Boulogne very well and could she help? By mistake, she addressed her package to the War Office, which happened to be in the midst of recruiting French operatives, and they immediately sent for her.

She was flown to France to help kick Gestapo ass, which she did with grace and gusto while also demonstrating a first-rate ability to withstand torture of any kind. When the Nazis captured her in a bid to extract vital Allied intelligence, she refused to surrender even an ounce of information. Her back was scorched with hot iron rods, her toenails were painfully pulled out one by one, but Odette remained fiercely tight-lipped. Eventually, the Germans gave up, threw her into solitary confinement and completely failed to win the war, thanks in part to Odette's almighty resistance work and capacity to endure even the toughest torture.

* Aka *that* dress worn by Liz Hurley.

BADASS RATING: ★★★★
A national heroine and all-round badass spy.

OLGA

Will your daughter be strong, savvy and a little bit scary? Then name her after the Russian princess and powerhouse who fought back with a posse of pigeons, Olga of Kiev (*c*.890–969).

When the Drevlyans murdered her husband, Prince Igor of Kiev, Olga became the ruler of the Rus. But the Drevlyans were not best pleased about a woman holding power, so they sent a group of their best men to negotiate a marriage between Olga and their own choice of king. This was their first mistake.

Olga, a strong and fearless monarch, was not about to take any shit from a group of twenty-something Drevlyan ambassadors who rocked up to her door doing their best Cilla Black act – especially not from those responsible for the death of her beloved.

So she ordered her army to dig a giant trench, and proceeded to boot every one of the Drevlyan matchmakers into the ditch, then buried them alive.

Revenge isn't something to be done half-assed and Olga didn't stop there. When more Drevlyans arrived, she locked them in a bathhouse and scorched them to death. Her army then stormed into the enemy city and took out over 5,000 Drevlyans. While those remaining begged for mercy, Olga launched a mob of pigeons, all with sulphur cloths bound to their claws; as each pigeon flew to its nest, it set it ablaze, and the city burnt to the ground.

BADASS RATING: ★★★
Don't mess with Olga.

OLIVE

Will your little scribbler be clever, courageous and creative? Then name her after the free-thinking political rebel and novelist, Olive Emilie Albertina Schreiner (1855–1920).

Born a missionary's daughter in the Eastern Cape in South Africa, Olive was angered by her parents' philosophy that women were born simply to procreate and pander to the patriarchy. She was also 100 per cent not down with British imperialism in South Africa, and subsequently dedicated much of her life to campaigning for social justice and equality.

Olive flipped the bird to convention and became a writer. She created unconventional heroines – those who were strong, who did not conform and who stood up for the rights of women. Her most renowned novel and one of the famous early feminist texts, *The Story of an African Farm*, became an instant bestseller despite causing major controversy for its casual portrayal of atheism, premarital sex, pregnancy and cross-dressing. Pretty progressive stuff for 1883, but then Olive was no ordinary woman, and in her personal warfare against oppression, she knew the pen was mightier than the sword.

BADASS RATING: ★ ★ ★ ★
A pioneering feminist and literary legend.

L'OLONNAIS

Want to inspire your little tiger to stand up for himself in this great, big world? Then name him after the brutal booty-swindling buccaneer, who ruthlessly roared across the high seas, François L'Olonnais (*c*.1630–69).

You didn't mess with L'Olonnais. He was born to an impoverished French family – so broke that he was banished to Spain to work as a slave. The Spaniards weren't the kindest of masters to poor young L'Olonnais and he built up a teeny bit of resentment towards them. So when he reinvented himself as a pirate, can you guess who was on his hit list?

Known for removing the tongues of traitors, slicing off large chunks of flesh from those he disliked, tossing anyone disrespectful overboard and cutting out and then eating the heart of an enemy, it is safe to say that L'Olonnais, over the years, had really learnt to defend himself.

BADASS RATING: ★
The cut-throat pirate who pretty much beheaded every Spaniard he met.

Oprah

Want to inspire your daughter to be true to herself? Then name her after the firecracker, first ever female African-American TV host, prodigious philanthropist and self-made billionaire, Oprah Winfrey (b.1954).

Raised in rural Mississippi, Oprah overcame adversity to steal the hearts of Americans as the most legendary, generous and fearless chat show host of all time. Her childhood was not easy, but that didn't stop Oprah following her dreams and completely owning it. From anchoring the evening news at her local radio station at nineteen years old to making a fledgling TV chat show so successful they renamed it after her, Oprah shook up the world with her straight-talking, no-nonsense and seriously cool badassitude. She wasn't afraid to talk about the taboo – homosexuality, drug addiction, abuse – and always did so with compassion and kindness.

A heart on her sleeve wearer, a good news bearer and with a generosity that knows no bounds, Oprah's many charities are entirely self-funded. She instigated and established a bill to help make America's children safer, and she is a fierce champion of the power of the people.

Badass quote: 'It doesn't matter who you are, where you come from. The ability to triumph begins with you. Always.'

BADASS RATING: ★★★★★
Basically one of the most awesome humans on the planet. Hail Queen Oprah!

Orson

Will your future son be blessed with unruly talents? Then name him after the riotous renegade, maverick filmmaker and adored actor, Orson Welles (1915–85).

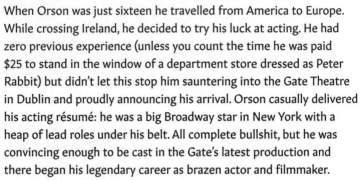

When Orson was just sixteen he travelled from America to Europe. While crossing Ireland, he decided to try his luck at acting. He had zero previous experience (unless you count the time he was paid $25 to stand in the window of a department store dressed as Peter Rabbit) but didn't let this stop him sauntering into the Gate Theatre in Dublin and proudly announcing his arrival. Orson casually delivered his acting résumé: he was a big Broadway star in New York with a heap of lead roles under his belt. All complete bullshit, but he was convincing enough to be cast in the Gate's latest production and there began his legendary career as brazen actor and filmmaker.

Orson's first film, *Citizen Kane*, which he wrote, produced, directed and starred in, went on to become known as one of the greatest films ever made. A Hollywood outsider and an illusionist, Orson is hailed as one of the most genius filmmakers in history.

BADASS RATING: ★★★
An enigma, an innovator and tour de force with extravagant talent.

Orwell

Will your son grow up determined to speak his own mind and be unafraid to challenge tyranny? Then name him after the fascist-fighting, totalitarian-tussling, liberalism-lobbying literary legend and champion of free speech, George Orwell (1903–50).

Born in India but educated in England, Orwell sacked off school before moving to Burma to join the Indian Imperial Police, where he grew a mean moustache, got several tattoos and spent his days stomping the streets combating crime, acting as personal bodyguard for over 250,000 civilians and perfecting the art of badassery.

When the Spanish Civil War broke out, he volunteered to fight alongside the Republicans before suffering a near-fatal shot to the throat, somehow surviving and escaping the country just before Soviet spies had him assassinated.

He then moved to London, took up the slightly less death-defying job of arts reviewer and knocked out a couple of books based on his experiences, including *Animal Farm*, a cautionary tale about totalitarianism, which became an instant bestseller.

Death finally did catch up with Orwell, and it was during the cold sweats and delirium of his final months, when he was suffering from tuberculosis, that he wrote *1984* – a terrifying, dystopic peek into the future, which is basically the greatest novel in history.

BADASS RATING: ★★★★★
Honest, insightful and bona fide badass.

Osceola

Will your future son be brave? Then name him after the Indian who battled tirelessly to protect Native North American territory, Osceola (1804–38).

When General Andrew Jackson and his troops invaded the Red Stick Creeks in Alabama in 1814, Osceola and his mother fled to Florida and took refuge with the Native American tribe known as the Seminoles. Osceola spent the next few years honing his survival skills so that when Jackson showed up in Florida, he was ready to stand up and tell the general to 'back the fuck off Indian land'.

So began a long war between the Native Americans and the US army. When other Seminole chiefs were persuaded to sign a treaty of removal, Osceola showed the US army exactly what he thought of their negotiations by plunging his knife into the paper. He then blew the brains out of the agent tasked with the removal of the Seminole tribe, and proceeded to beat the shit out of any general who dared to step foot on Seminole land.

From fighting across alligator-infested waters to ambushing enemy soldiers in the dead of night, Osceola led his tribe to victory after victory. After three years of resistance, he was eventually defeated and imprisoned, but his place in history as one of the greatest Native American warriors of all time had already been marked.

BADASS RATING: ★★★★
A revered hero who fought for freedom and justice.

MORE OUTRAGEOUS Os

ODETTA

Odetta Holmes (1930–2008) was a trailblazing American folk legend whose voice became the soundtrack of the civil rights movement.

BADASS RATING: ★ ★ ★ ★

OLAVE

Olave Baden-Powell (1889–1977), pioneer of the Girl Guides, was an all-round good egg – a fearless adventurer, intrepid traveller and a doyenne of good deeds.

BADASS RATING: ★ ★ ★

OLE

Ole Kirk Christiansen (1891–1958) – the dude invented LEGO.

BADASS RATING: ★ ★

MORE OUTRAGEOUS Os

OMU

Omu Okwei (1872–1943), hailed as the 'Merchant Queen of Osomari', sailed the Niger river selling clothing, pans and household goods. She became one of Nigeria's richest women.

BADASS RATING: ★★★

ORVILLE

Orville Wright (1871–1948) was the pioneering American aviator and inventor who built and flew the very first engine-powered aeroplane.

BADASS RATING: ★★★

OTTOLINE

Ottoline Morrell (1873–1938) was a society hostess of the early twentieth century and muse to many early-twentieth-century writers, from D. H. Lawrence to Virginia Woolf.

BADASS RATING: ★★

PÁDRAIG

Can you feel a little revolutionist growing in your womb, one that might march his way out, burn the shackles of suppression and inspire a global liberation movement? Then name him after ultimate rebel and iconic hero of Irish history, Pádraig Henry Pearse (1879–1916).

Pádraig led the 1916 Easter Rising, a revolt against British power in Ireland. After two years of secret planning to launch a strategically timed attack, Pádraig triumphantly flipped the bird to the British Empire. This ultimate act of rebellion may have cost him his life, but it set the path for Irish independence and a movement across the world for liberation from the clutches of the Brits. Pádraig famously declared, 'When we are all wiped out, people will blame us... but in a few years they will see the meaning of what we tried to do.'

A champion of the Irish language, Gaeilge, he also wrote Irish poetry, founded Irish-speaking schools and fought to save Gaeilge from extinction.

Badass fact: A shilling bears his bust – Pádraig is the only political figure to appear on Irish currency.

BADASS RATING: ★★★
A rebel who sacrificed his life to change the world.

PAMELA

Want your little wren to believe in her own divinity? Then name her after the queen of living life to the M-A-X, Pamela Des Barres (b.1948).

Famous for her intimate relationships with Frank Zappa, Keith Moon, Jimi Hendrix and Jim Morrison, Pamela was the ultimate party animal. In fact, partying with her was much like throwing shapes with a sequined unicorn on speed. As a teenager, Pamela had the balls to barge her way to the front of a crowd to gaze adoringly into the eyes of the lead guitarist at pretty much every gig she attended. Later she would hot-foot it to the band's hotel, brazenly knock on the door and invite herself in to the after-party of a lifetime. Then get up and go to school the next day, because throwing naked shapes with Mick Jagger was just another Tuesday night.

When she graduated from high school, Pamela engineered casual work so she could live near Sunset Strip and dedicate 100 per cent of her efforts to the heady pursuit of rock. She turned up at gigs in nothing more than a pair of suspenders, rode motorbikes down hotel corridors, hallucinated erupting 'towers of lime-green sherbet' and occasionally felt the wrath of the long-suffering girlfriends. She went from fan girl to friend of the stars, styled Alice Cooper and formed her own band called Girls Together Outrageously; then she married musician Michael Des Barres, bashed out a couple of bestselling memoirs on her fearless rock 'n' roll adventures and put her party feet up for a well-earned rest.*

* Just kidding. Pamela is still going like a bejewelled unicorn on speed.

BADASS RATING: ★★
Forever remembered for banging a bunch of rock gods, no one can accuse Pamela of not having lived her best life.

PANCHO

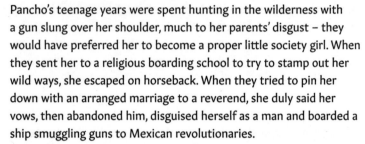

Want to inspire your little squidge to live life by her own rules? Then name her after Hollywood's first female stunt pilot, Pancho Barnes (1901–75).

Pancho's teenage years were spent hunting in the wilderness with a gun slung over her shoulder, much to her parents' disgust – they would have preferred her to become a proper little society girl. When they sent her to a religious boarding school to try to stamp out her wild ways, she escaped on horseback. When they tried to pin her down with an arranged marriage to a reverend, she duly said her vows, then abandoned him, disguised herself as a man and boarded a ship smuggling guns to Mexican revolutionaries.

She then spent a few years throwing outrageous parties, smoking cigars, swearing like a trooper and generally living a life of excess. She also learnt to fly, declaring the exhilaration of aviation to be akin to a bloody good shag. She broke flight speed records, set up a company parachuting women out of planes, became the top aeronautical stuntwoman in America and generally behaved like a total boss.

BADASS RATING: ★ ★ ★ ★
An uncompromising badass who lived her life at full throttle.

PEARL

Will your future daughter be cool, determined and resourceful? Then name her after the French-British spy, Pearl Witherington Cornioley (1914–2008).

Pearl escaped to London from France in 1940. With her lover (and future husband) trapped in a Nazi concentration camp and her family torn apart, Pearl set about seeking revenge and helping the British with the war effort in any way possible. She joined the British Special Operations Executive and fast became the best shot – male or female – that they had ever seen. Extremely capable and courageous, Pearl was pretty all right with being dropped out of an aeroplane at great height, and could easily blind the enemy side with her intellect and charm; often posing as a travelling saleswoman to camouflage her ulterior motives.

Pearl was just twenty-nine when she parachuted into Nazi-occupied France. Here she set about creating fresh hell for the German army, disrupting a train line to Paris no less than 800 times. When the leader of her crew was caught by the Gestapo, Pearl took charge of over 3,500 French Resistance fighters. She commanded them with such panache that they utterly destroyed their German opponents and forced the surrender of 18,000 troops. Legend!

Recognizing that Pearl was 100 per cent badass, the Germans offered a million-franc reward for her capture. But they did not succeed. And when the war was over, Pearl set about getting revenge on the British government for failing to recognize her war efforts. When they eventually gave her an honour, she gave them the finger.

BADASS RATING: ★★★★
Nazi-slaying queen.

PEGGY

Is the little brain you are growing destined for greatness? Then take inspiration from the mathematical maverick who wrote the coding to land the first human beings on the moon, Margaret 'Peggy' Hamilton (b.1936).

An ardent lover of maths, Peggy was just thirty-three when she led the team of over a hundred engineers and coders that designed the software for NASA's Apollo programme.

   If that wasn't remarkable enough, she then singlehandedly rescued the 1969 moon landing mission from disaster by developing a code that saved everyone's ass. Peggy programmed the rocket's computer to recognize high-priority tasks over low-priority ones, which doesn't sound that impressive – until Neil A. and his gang were minutes away from docking on the moon and the rocket's alarm bells fired into action because its computer was completely overwhelmed with data, the result of a potentially fatal error triggered by one of the crew. But the panic was short-lived – the computer swiftly recognized the error thanks to Peggy's pioneering badassery, and NASA made space history.

BADASS RATING: ★ ★ ★ ★ ★
Self-taught programmer and trailblazer who changed the world.

PERCY

Want to inspire your little rogue to stand up for what he believes in? Then name him after the radical, controversial and epically talented poet, Percy Bysshe Shelley (1792–1822).

An atheist and anarchist, Percy was known in school as 'Mad Shelley' for his blatant aversion to authority. He was expelled from Oxford University for producing anti-establishment pamphlets, which he refused to deny authorship of; he believed in sexual and religious freedom, was a devout vegetarian and campaigned tirelessly for social equality, outing the greed of the rich and the oppression of the working class, which at the time was pretty progressive stuff.

When he fell in love with Mary Wollstonecraft, he casually suggested to his first wife, Harriet Westbrook, that she might be up for Mary moving into their digs and the three of them living together in free-loving, creative harmony. A bold move, which unsurprisingly Harriet was not up for, but you have to admire his bare-faced cheek.

BADASS RATING: ★★★
Revolutionary, reformer and one of the most influential poets of the nineteenth century.

PHILLIS

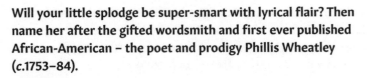

Will your little splodge be super-smart with lyrical flair? Then name her after the gifted wordsmith and first ever published African-American – the poet and prodigy Phillis Wheatley (*c*.1753–84).

Born in the Gambia, Phillis was kidnapped at seven years old, put on board a slave ship en route to America and never saw her family again. She was sold to the Wheatley family in Boston, who noticed she was bright, and went against convention in teaching her to read and allowing her to attend English, Latin and Greek lessons.

Phillis wrote her first published poem, 'On Messrs. Hussey and Coffin', when she was just thirteen, and by the age of sixteen she had gained fame from her literary works. At twenty, her poetry collection was published as a book, and Phillis made history as the first African-American (and third ever woman) to have words in print.

BADASS RATING: ★★★★
The boundary-busting badass who despite being bound by the shackles of slavery found a voice of her own.

PHILOTHEY

Will the little human you are growing be fiercely loyal and badass in a saintly kinda way? Then name her after the high-kicking, axe-wielding nun who would stop at nothing to protect her convent – Philothey Benizelos (*c.*1650).

Philothey established a nunnery in Greece in the 1650s. It grew quite a reputation as the hottest ticket in town and many sisters travelled great distances to join her cloister. They were educated, taught to fight, given weapons and if anyone gave the abbess any beef, the nuns came out and showed them who was boss.

Local village women also took refuge in her abbey, but this caused some distress to the local authorities who, fearing Philothey's growing power, decided to imprison her. Legend has it that she bribed a prison guard, faked her own murder and hot-footed it to a nearby town to live the rest of her life under a new identity.

BADASS RATING: ★★★
Don't mess with Philothey, nun-warrior and first-rate jailbreak.

PHOEBE

Reckon you've hit bullseye with your newest brood? Then name her after the expert shot, stuntwoman and star of the Wild West, Phoebe Ann Mosey – stage name Annie Oakley (1860–1926).

A crack shot with a side serving of sass, as a child Phoebe honed her shooting skills hunting squirrels in the backwoods of Ohio. So top-notch was her talent that by the time she was twelve, Phoebe had paid off her mother's mortgage from the money she made demonstrating her rifle tricks.

When the revered marksman and performer Frank Butler came to town, Phoebe challenged him to a duel. And of course kicked his ass. So Frank did what any smart man would do – he put a ring on it, and together husband and wife toured the world as part of Buffalo Bill's Wild West show.

Phoebe quickly became the company's highest earner. She could shoot a playing card in half through its thin edge, snuff out a candle with a single bullet, toss glass balls into the air and swiftly blast the shit out of them. She once blew a lit cigarette from the lips of Friedrich Wilhelm II in a single shot. Queen Victoria adored her; Chief Sitting Bull was so impressed with her superhuman skills that he adopted her, and Phoebe became a global icon. She also taught thousands of women self-defence, led an all-female fighting regiment during the Spanish-American War and generally acted like a total boss.

BADASS RATING: ★★★★★
The greatest sharpshooter the world has ever seen.

PHRYNE

Will your future daughter be born with a lotta sass? Then name her after the Athenian harlot known for her beauty, quick wit and wisdom as well as her free love – Phryne of Thespiae (*c.*370–*c.*316 BC).

Phryne was one of the richest women in Athens and entirely self-made. She had so much Ancient Greek dollar that she offered to pay to rebuild her city's crumbled walls after they were destroyed by Alexander the Great; but the city's authorities declined her charity. It was a pretty stupid move on their part, but given that Phryne's whole persona perfectly occupied the Venn diagram space between trashy whore and glamorous millionaire, many believe that they refused to be bankrolled by a call girl on principle.

Phryne is legendary for many acts of brazen badassery, but one that really stands out is the time she found herself on the wrong end of a lawsuit. As the trial was coming to a close and her defence lawyer had been worse than useless, the quick-thinking Phryne decided to prove her divinity and whipped out her juggernauts for the judge and jury to see. It turned out these particular assets were welcome in the court of Ancient Greece, and after much exclamation over her mind-blowing breasts ('She must be holy – they are a gift from God!') the guys swiftly acquitted her. Epic!

BADASS RATING: ★★★
The fireball who flashed her way to freedom (and made a total mockery of the Athenian legal system in doing so).

POLICARPA

Will your daughter have champion courage? Then name her after the Colombian heroine who spied for revolutionary forces, Policarpa Salavarrieta (*c.*1791–1817).

During Colombia's war of independence, Policarpa and her brother forged the necessary documents to enter the city of Bogotá on a mission to gather vital intelligence for rebel leaders. Assuming a new identity, Policarpa offered her services as seamstress to unsuspecting loyalist families. She would cross-stitch away in their homes while listening out for new information; from delving through personal papers to gathering maps, planned military movement and lists of those suspected of revolt, Policarpa was the perfect sleuth. She also recruited locals to join the anti-Spanish revolutionary movement and bought a shitload of weapons to kick Spanish ass. Although she was ultimately found and hanged for treason, her plight inspired radical resistance; she has now become a great symbol of bravery and courage in Colombia.

BADASS RATING: ★★★★
A celebrated hero of independence.

PYTHAGORAS

Will your little noggin be a deep-thinking numbers whizz? Then name him after the Greek mathematician and philosopher, Pythagoras (*c.*570–495 BC).

Renowned for developing the beloved formula that calculates the length of the long side of a right-angled triangle, Pythagoras did more than just provide a staple module in every child's maths education. He was a vegetable-worshipping mystical leader, a number-obsessive and one of the earliest influencers in maths and philosophy. During his lifetime, his mind-blowing genius became so famous that he had his very own superfan club – a bunch of blokes known as the Pythagoreans who followed him across the globe. The initiation into their own self-formed geek squad was a five-year vow of silence, and they were so in awe of Pythagoras's mathematical genius that they convinced each other he was a gift from God.

BADASS RATING: ★★★★
Numerical demi-god and all-round wise wizard whose revelations changed the world.

MORE PHENOMENAL Ps

PABLO

Pablo Picasso (1881–1973) was one of the twentieth century's most influential artists, with a penchant for goats, the colour blue and giving zero fucks.

BADASS RATING: ★★★

PATTI

Patti Smith (b.1946) is a musical visionary with a mystical, sod-the-system attitude that has earned her the title Godmother of Punk.

BADASS RATING: ★★★★

PAUL

Paul Gascoigne (b.1967), one of England's greatest footballers, will forever be remembered and adored for becoming more than a little moist in the eye during the 1990 World Cup semi-final.

BADASS RATING: ★

MORE PHENOMENAL Ps

PEDRO

Pedro Menéndez de Avilés (1519–74) was the swashbuckling Spanish privateer and intrepid adventurer who discovered Florida.

BADASS RATING: ★

PETRA

Petra Herrera (b. *c.*1890) was a Mexican revolutionary who disguised herself as a man called Pedro to join the army and lead a siege on the town of Torreón.

BADASS RATING: ★ ★ ★ ★

PLATO

Plato (423–348 BC) was a classical Greek philosopher and founder of the Academy in Athens, one of the earliest-known schools.

BADASS RATING: ★ ★ ★ ★

MORE PHENOMENAL Ps

PRATHIA

Prathia Hall (1940–2002), boundary-busting, barrier-breaking preacher and civil rights leader, inspired Martin Luther King's speech 'I have a Dream'.

BADASS RATING: ★★★★

PYTHIAS

Pythias (362–326 BC) was a trailblazing Ancient Greek biologist with a specimen collection that would make the archives of the Natural History Museum look like a science teacher's storeroom.

BADASS RATING: ★★★★

QUENTIN

Will your squishious little human bean be brimming with creativity? Then name him after a total bell-ringer, the phizz-whizzing, whoopsy-splunker and treasured illustrator, Quentin Saxby Blake (b.1932).

With his imaginative, zany drawings and uniquely puckish style, Quentin has made a legendary career as an illustrator and author. His first ever paid job was for the satirical magazine *Punch* at the age of sixteen; moving on to collaborate with Roald Dahl for many decades and create his most celebrated characters, Quentin has illustrated over 300 books.

   Often employing an inked-up quill pen made from a vulture feather as the tool of his trade, Quentin's artwork catapults from the page with daring delights. He has created the snarling mouths of child-hating witches; wings of mythical monsters; the dream jar in the *BFG*; and that scene in *Matilda* where a pupil finds himself on the wrong end of Miss Trunchbull's foot and is flung outside through the classroom window.

   Described as drawing with a 'whoosh', Quentin's spunky and spontaneous artwork has become a staple in every child's library.

BADASS RATING: ★★★
Britain's beloved illustrator and a casual genius.

QUINCY

Will your future son be badass to the bone with immense talent? Name him after prolific musician and producer and 100 per cent legit legend, Quincy Jones (b.1933).

Nominated for seventy-nine Grammys and with twenty-seven wins, Quincy has worked with a bunch of banging musicians from Ray Charles and Billie Holiday to Aretha Franklin. He collaborated with Frank Sinatra; produced Michael Jackson's albums and transformed the world with *Thriller*; launched the careers of Oprah Winfrey and Will Smith, to name a few. His music was the first played on the moon; he wrote for Steven Spielberg; he was executive producer for *The Fresh Prince of Bel-Air* (and composed *that* theme tune) and has basically owned the music industry since he first rocked onto the scene as a jazz trumpeter and bandleader at the age of eighteen.

Born on the south side of Chicago, Quincy's childhood consisted of dodging situations where he might end up on the wrong side of a switchblade. He briefly lived it up in a shotgun shack in Louisville, fended off hunger with a diet of cooked rats, and his early years were generally spent defying death and danger in equal measure. Quincy was the only surviving passenger in a car crash with a Trailways bus when he was just a teen, and he gave death the finger once more when he was diagnosed with a couple of brain aneurysms and given a 1 in 100 chance of survival. He has since lived to double the age predicted.

BADASS RATING: ★★★★★
A master inventor who has revolutionized the music industry.

ANOTHER QUALITY Q

QUEENIE

Queenie McKenzie (1915–98) was a forthright, energetic and immensely talented Indigenous Australian artist and activist. Declared a 'State Living Treasure' in the year of her death, Queenie used natural earth pigments to create landscapes that are now exhibited in galleries across the globe.

BADASS RATING: ★★★

RANAVALONA

Want to give your daughter a name that really packs a punch? No one is going to mess with the namesake of the most murderous queen in history, Ranavalona-Manjaka (1778–1861).

Bat-shit crazy Ranavalona rose to power in Madagascar after her husband died a suspiciously sudden and early death. Not the natural heir to the throne, Ranavalona secured her reign through a series of epic slaughters on most of the remaining monarchy. To her credit, once she was officially the boss lady, she repelled all French and British forces from Madagascar with great efficiency and ensured her country remained fiercely independent. Down with colonizers!

Ranavalona kick-started Madagascar's industrial revolution and continued to slay anyone who dared to cross her path. In fact, she took her slaying to a whole new level; in increasingly creative and insane ways, she managed to wipe out half the population. She crushed testicles in a vice; coated her own feet in poison and forced her enemies to kiss them to death; she often liked to boil people alive. Ranavalona's psychotic murderous methods make Rosemary West look like a nice person.

BADASS RATING: ★
Anyone who gave this chick beef was blown to hell.

RASPUTIN

Will your future son be invincible and self-assured? Then name him after the Russian wonder and mystic, Grigori Rasputin (1869–1916).

From peasant to prophet and revered healer to the Romanov dynasty, Rasputin was a self-proclaimed 'Christ in miniature'. And anyone that sure of their own divinity is kinda badass. He took it up a level by proclaiming that his debauched lifestyle (involving copious amounts of booze and banging) and aversion to soap (the guy was in serious need of a good clean) were all part of spiritual suffering, and this gave him free rein to do whatever he liked.

Aside from his magical powers in healing sick horses and children, all while predicting the future, Rasputin is known for being completely impossible to kill. When a group of conspirators decided it was time for him to meet his end, they gave him a lethal dose of poison. This didn't work. So they shot him in the back, twice in the head and pounded him with a rubber truncheon, just to be sure. This also didn't work. As a last resort, they tied him in cloth, attached a lead weight and dumped him in a freezing river. Rumour has it he clawed back through the ice and emerged resurrected.

BADASS RATING: ★★★
Religious mystic with superhuman powers.

REINHOLD

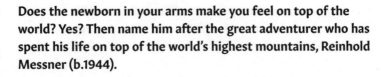

Does the newborn in your arms make you feel on top of the world? Yes? Then name him after the great adventurer who has spent his life on top of the world's highest mountains, Reinhold Messner (b.1944).

Reinhold climbed his first mountain at five years old. He went from conquering a casual 3,300-metre Geisler in his homeland in northeastern Italy to adventuring across the world, hitting the highest summits with increasing amounts of badassery.

Reinhold was the first man to climb all fourteen mountains on earth that have a summit classified as a 'death zone', which means they're over 8,000 metres high and there's more than a reasonable chance of pegging out at the peak, as it were.

Reinhold was also the first man to climb Mount Everest without the use of an oxygen canister. At the time (1978) scientists had concluded that the high altitude of Everest's summit could cause irreversible brain damage (best case) or death (worst case, assumed), so off Reinhold trotted. While his climbing partner, Peter Habeler, had liquid pouring from every orifice of his body after an unfortunate incident with a tin of spoiled sardines, Reinhold attempted the last leg of the summit. A storm came. Reinhold made his second attempt, this time with his recovered buddy, and a brutal climb and a few terrific altitude-induced hallucinations later, they reached the peak of Everest. A triumph for mankind, and of insanity.

BADASS RATING: ★ ★ ★ ★ ★
The world's most fearless mountaineer.

RENÉ

**Want to inspire your future son to live out his best life?
Then name him after the brainbox with serious swagger –
philosopher and scientist, René Descartes (1596–1650).**

René shunned the work of previous philosophers in favour of his
own maverick approach, which kinda got the goat of his fellow
academics, but delivered some pretty A1 breakthroughs in the fields
of maths and philosophy. He solved the unsolvable (geometric
problem) by inventing the entire field of analytical geometry; he
inspired a generation of rational sceptics, and did a bunch of other
ground-breaking stuff.

René's views were deemed so radical the pope banned the
printing of his publications and placed all his work on the Index
of Prohibited Books, which only served to make him appear even
more badass.

Aside from his giant mind grapes, there are many other reasons
to admire René: he never got out of bed before 11 a.m.; his wardrobe
was first-rate; and he came up with the gem, 'I think, therefore I am,'
after shutting himself in an oven for five days, because that is exactly
how an offbeat genius like René liked to roll. . .

BADASS RATING: ★★★
The father of modern philosophy.

RIMBAUD

Is that a look of disdain coming from the little alien-like face in your ultrasound picture? Then name your child Rimbaud after the angriest poet of all time, Jean Nicolas Arthur Rimbaud (1854–91).

Considering Rimbaud was too furious to write any more poetry after the age of twenty-one, his canon of work is pretty impressive. In a few short years he managed to convey his contempt for capitalism, patriotism, society and pretty much everything that is fucked-up or wrong with the world in a body of work that went on to inspire an entire literary movement.

Rimbaud's adolescence was spent repeatedly running away from his domineering mother, while developing his own unique writing style. His first poem was published at fifteen; by seventeen he was living as a beggar on the streets of Paris; and by eighteen he was riding the highs and lows of a stormy love affair with fellow poet Paul Verlaine. Together the two lovers inhaled insane amounts of illegal stimulants and hard liquor with a lust for life that saw Paul Verlaine end the relationship in the most ceremonious of ways. He got drunk, charged into Rimbaud's hotel room and shot at him. Twice.

BADASS RATING: ★★★
A shocking and exhilarating poet who also had great punk hair before punk rock was even a thing.

RIVER

Is the kid preparing his grand entrance going to be so cool that even you are a little bit intimidated? Then name him after the actor, icon and free-wheeling heartthrob who scores an A++++ on the awesome scale, River Phoenix (1970–93).

Born to real-deal flowers-in-the-hair, free-spirited hippies, River's original name was the slightly less exotic River Jude Bottom. The family adopted the new surname Phoenix when they joined a religious sect called the Children of God and decided it was time for a rebrand. River and his siblings were the kind of free-range, self-taught, devoutly vegan, busk-on-the-street-for-supper epically cool beings.

From his first major part in the film *Stand by Me* to his Oscar nomination for *Running on Empty*, River stormed Hollywood, guitar in hand, ready to shred the shit out of it and life. He also had hair worthy of a Herbal Essence commercial and made all the girls swoon.

BADASS RATING: ★★★★
Too cool for this life.

ROALD

Make your little sprog the namesake of two legends for the price of one. Name him after the fearless adventurer who was so friggin' awesome, Roald Dahl's parents famously chose his moniker for their newborn son – Roald Amundsen (1872–1928).

An intrepid Norwegian explorer, Roald Amundsen led expeditions to the last few unknown regions of the world. He was first to the Northwest Passage, first to successfully cross the Arctic by air (first to reach the North Pole, according to some) and most famously, the first human being ever to conquer the South Pole.

It takes a brave man to journey into a wilderness so insanely cold that it can barely support life. And an even braver man to try it for the second time after –80 degree temperatures forced him to abort his first attempt.

For almost two months, Roald and his crew of men, dogs and sledges travelled more than 1,300 kilometres over rugged, uncharted terrain. They scaled frozen glaciers, withstood raging blizzards, fought off wild animals and got so hungry that at one point they had to kill and eat their own dogs. The sub-zero Antarctic weather was so crazy that the huskies that hadn't been sacrificed to fend off starvation pretty much froze to death anyway, but Roald pushed on. On 14 December 1911, he become the first person to reach the southernmost point on earth.

BADASS RATING: ★★★★
A daring voyager of the highest rank.

ROSA

Is your little bud ready to start a revolution? Then name her after the revered writer, Marxist philosopher and activist, Rosa Luxemburg (1871–1919).

Rosa was 100 per cent bona fide badass. She was exiled from Poland at the age of eighteen for her progressive political views. In Berlin she became a key figurehead for the largest radical party in the world, the German Social Democratic Party. She combined this with being a first-rate lecturer in economics – no mean feat for a woman living in the latter half of the nineteenth century.

Rosa was fiercely against Germany's role in the First World War and was jailed for several years for her campaigning. But a few iron bars did not stop Rosa's anti-war, stick-it-to-the-man crusade and she spent her time inside writing pamphlets and delivering informal lectures in the prison canteen.

Rosa founded the Spartacus League, a group of badass ninjas who called for social reform, and in 1918 she established the German Communist Party. It was created in the hope of ending the First World War through an anti-capitalist revolt, and gathered significant momentum. Rosa sacrificed her life in the fight for her principles.

BADASS RATING: ★★★★
Philosopher, political leader and one of the twentieth century's greatest revolutionaries.

ROSITA

Will your future daughter be called by the gods of wanderlust? Then name her after the daring English adventurer, Rosita Forbes (1890–1967).

Like most women in Victorian England, Rosita married young. After a few years of unfulfilling matrimony, she decided there was more to life than domestic drudgery, so she left her husband, pawned her wedding ring and used the money to embark on the gap year of a lifetime.

From the Sahara to Samarkand, Rosita trekked across the desert, climbed mountains, navigated wild seas and rode thousands of miles on horseback. She visited some thirty countries between 1918 and 1919, writing about her travels in a number of publications. To fuel further voyages, Rosita then worked as journalist, a lecturer and documentary filmmaker while also knocking out about thirty books to inspire future generations to go forth and seek adventure.

BADASS RATING: ★ ★ ★ ★
A legendary explorer and travel writer.

RUBY

Will your little champ be brave, strong and determined? Then name her Ruby after the young girl whose courage and perseverance helped pave the way to the end of racial segregation across America – Ruby Nell Bridges (b.1954).

In 1960 Ruby was one of six children in New Orleans to pass the deliberately difficult aptitude test to attend an all-white school. The exam, which she was encouraged to sit by the National Association for the Advancement of Colored People, was made almost impossible by the state's government to enable them to keep the racial divide in their educational system for a few years longer. But Ruby was smart and she nailed it, which kind of showed them.

She boldly chose to attend the all-white William Franz Elementary and became the first African-American student to step through the school gates, rightly asserting her entitlement to an equal education. Angry mobs lined the entrance; a woman threatened to poison her; parents pulled their children out of her class; and Ruby had to be escorted by several marshals for her own safety. She was just six years old, but her extraordinary bravery sparked a change that rippled across New Orleans, empowering social justice and promoting tolerance.

As Ruby continued to turn up to school each morning, unafraid and undaunted by the resistance of those around her, attitudes shifted and the next year Ruby was joined by more African-American students.

BADASS RATING: ★★★★
One brave act of badassery that empowered and inspired others to end racial segregation in America.

RULON

Is your newest brood invincible? Then name him after the death-defying Olympic gold medallist and wrestling champion, Rulon Gardner (b.1971).

Rulon's first brush with death was at school, when a class show-and-tell took a sinister turn and an arrow from his classmate's crossbow was accidentally fired, impaling him. Having survived a junior re-enactment of a scene in *Braveheart*, Rulon then found himself battling the sub-zero temperatures of the Bridger-Teton National Forest when a snowmobile jolly with a couple of buddies left him stranded in the wilderness for seventeen hours. Hoping to reach the top of a steep mountain, Rulon had persevered despite losing his friends a few turns back. When his snowmobile drove off a 15-metre cliff and he was thrown from the wreckage, Rulon simply brushed himself down and waded through waist-high ice-cold water before camping out for the night wrapped in a soggy sock and praying to God that by some miracle he might be rescued.

With one toe fewer and fully recovered from a severe case of frostbite, Rulon gave death the finger once more when a car ploughed into his motorcycle.

Then, several years later, he was on board an aeroplane when it crashed into a lake, leaving him with the task of swimming for an hour to dry land and camping out once more in sub-zero temperatures. Of course, Rulon survived, because he is indestructible.

BADASS RATING: ★★★★
100 per cent unbreakable.

MORE REBEL Rs

RALPH

Ralph Stout (d. *c.*1697) was a fearless pirate who led a record number of mutinies. On announcing his retirement from piracy, his crew were so distraught they killed him.

BADASS RATING: ★ ★ ★

REGGIE

Reggie Walker (1889–1951) was the South African athlete in the 1908 Olympic Games who, at 19 years and 128 days, became (and remains) the youngest person ever to win the men's 100m gold.

BADASS RATING: ★ ★ ★

RITA

Rita Levi-Montalcini (1909–2012) defied her father by going to university, and went on to become an Italian Nobel laureate.

BADASS RATING: ★ ★ ★ ★ ★

MORE REBEL Rs

ROBIN

Robin Cavendish (1930–94) was a polio survivor who made it his mission to fight for the rights of disabled people.

BADASS RATING: ★★★★★

ROSALIND

Rosalind Franklin (1920–58) was the super-smart British scientist who discovered DNA. She took the first photo of DNA, now referred to as Photo 51.

BADASS RATING: ★★★★

ROSE

Rose Schneiderman (1882–1972), American activist and labour union leader, championed the rights of the working class, the poor and women's suffrage.

BADASS RATING: ★★★★

MORE REBEL Rs

ROY

Roy Sullivan (1912–83) was the American park ranger who was struck by lightning seven times and survived. Damn Gina!

BADASS RATING: ★★★★

SARAH

Want to inspire your little one to forge her own path and follow her dreams? Then name her after the original Mum boss and first female African-American millionaire, Sarah Breedlove, aka Madam C. J. Walker (1867–1919).

When Sarah's husband died young and she found herself a single mum, penniless and suffering with hair loss, she took matters into her own hands. She researched recipes and techniques to produce a range of homemade hair care products designed especially for black hair. From humble beginnings in her Louisiana kitchen to selling her tress-taming treatments across America, Sarah created an empire so successful that in a few short years its income was nearly $5 million.

Aside from buying a couple of lavish mansions, Sarah mostly gave her money away to those in need. She funded educational scholarships for women, established the first YMCA in Indianapolis and became a patron of the Harlem Renaissance.

BADASS RATING: ★★★★★
From the cotton fields to owning half of Manhattan, Sarah was a trailblazing entrepreneur who used her wealth to change the world.

Seabury

Will your wormling embrace the weird and wonderful? Then name him after the unique writer and purveyor of strange, Seabury Quinn (1889–1969).

A pioneer in horror fiction, Quinn wrote over 200 short stories and a bunch of scare-the-pants-off-you novels alongside his day job as mortuary lawyer and editor of the trade magazine *Casket & Sunnyside* (no jokes). His most famous work stars the supernatural detective Jules de Grandin, known as 'the occult Hercules Poirot' – a crime-busting French doctor who takes on werewolves, the dead and the insane in pursuit of the truth. Creating everything from spooks and zombies to sex-changing Egyptologists, Quinn blazed balls-out into unconventional realms to write wildly bold and outrageous stories.

BADASS RATING: ★ ★
Marched to the beat of a different drum, like a boss.

SERGE

Will your future son be cheeky, outlandish and full of vigour? Then name him after the Parisian pop poet, louche lyrical legend and purveyor of the provocative, Serge Gainsbourg (1928–91).

A genius who made pop music into an art form, Serge swaggered through life with a casual disregard for all convention and conformity. From performing the reggae version of the French national anthem to creating one of the most banned radio songs in the world, Serge was known as subversive, charismatic and, quite simply, not giving a damn.

His records were unashamedly salacious. He once hung a microphone from his bedpost to capture the sound of his most intimate moment and then nonchalantly seeded his authentic mating grunts onto his latest album release. His single 'Je t'aime… Moi non plus' was deemed too explicit for broadcast because it featured a woman orgasming. Despite this, it went on to become Number One in Europe and sell millions across the world.

Serge would think nothing of mouthing wild obscenities during public appearances, or propositioning whomever the hell he liked (Whitney Houston, once, live on national television). Eyebrows shot up when he performed a duet with his twelve-year-old daughter called 'Lemon Incest', and he famously burnt a 500-franc note on French TV in protest against high taxes. Atta boy!

BADASS RATING: ★★★★
A tantalizing troubadour of brilliance who shocked and awed the world in equal measure.

SHI

Will your little butterfly be a master of disguise? Then name him after the Chinese opera singer turned spy who led one of the most insane espionage missions in history, Shi Pei Pu (1938–2009).

Shi was an artist of minor celebrity status in China. He first met Bernard Boursicot, an unsuspecting twenty-year-old French diplomat, at a party in Beijing in 1964. Shi was a man, so it is no surprise that at the party he both looked and dressed like a man. However, he let Bernard into a secret – that he was in fact a woman, but to appease his controlling father, who had only wished for a son, he dressed as a man. Bernard was probably on his fifth cocktail by this point, so it all seemed quite plausible.

The two became friends and then lovers – Bernard still, quite unbelievably, believing that Shi was a woman. In an affair that lasted twenty years, Shi not only kept up the bonkers disguise, he/she also managed to copy hundreds of important diplomatic documents and hand them over to the Chinese.

BADASS RATING: ★★
A performer who created one of the most outrageous illusions in the history of espionage.

SID

Can you hear the sounds of anarchy echoing up from your pregnant belly? Then take inspiration from the lawless musician who pushed punk (and life) to its absolute limits, Sid Vicious (1957–79).

Sid rose to fame as the bassist for legendary British punk band The Sex Pistols. Everything the establishment stood for, Sid stood against. In his whole life, from his troubled childhood on a council estate in London to headlining in the biggest arenas across the globe, Sid was controversial, self-disruptive and an A1 rebel.

Badass quote: Undermine their pompous authority, reject their moral standards, make anarchy and disorder your trademarks. Cause as much disruption as possible but don't let them take you ALIVE!'

BADASS RATING: ★★
One of the world's most iconic punk figures.

SIDNEY

Will your future son have zero sense of danger? Then name him after the legendary Russian double agent hailed as the 'Ace of the Spies', Sidney Reilly (*c.*1874–1925).

Arrested for working as a messenger for a Marxist group, Sidney casually faked his own death and jumped on board a ship to South America. Rebranding himself as Pedro the Brazilian, he got a job as a cook on a British mission and then proceeded to save everyone's ass when local tribes attacked. One of the members of the mission happened to be a British agent, who, on seeing this audacious act of badassery, decided this guy would make a good spy. Once he learnt Sidney's real identity he was even more convinced.

Sidney worked as a freelance agent in Britain before returning to Russia to become a double agent for first the Japanese and then the Russians. Bankrolled by three major powers, Sidney was revered for his charisma, lavish lifestyle, speaking a tonne of languages and basically being really, really, really good at his job.

It was Sidney who provided the Japanese with the vital intelligence that allowed them to torpedo the shit out of the Russian navy at Port Arthur in 1904. He also shared Germany's warship blueprints with the British and carried out hundreds of other daring acts of espionage that had a massive influence on world history.

BADASS RATING: ★★★★
The real-life James Bond.

SIMONE

Will your future daughter be daring? Then name her after the French freedom fighter, Simone Segouin (b.1925).

At eighteen years old, Simone joined the Francs-Tireurs et Partisans – a group of communists and French nationalists hell-bent on resisting Nazi occupation in France during the Second World War. From her first mission of hijacking Gestapo pushbikes to stomping the streets of Paris with a machine-gun slung under her arm, Simone wreaked havoc in Germany. She blew up bridges, dodged near-death experiences and singlehandedly captured a few dozen German soldiers, ensuring they remained prisoners of war until France was liberated.

Simone won a bunch of medals for her derring-do, became a paediatric nurse and received the grand honour of having a Parisian street named after her – that's when you know you have really made it…

BADASS RATING: ★
An icon of the French resistance.

SOJOURNER

Hear the almighty roar of a strong, fierce lioness reverberating from your womb? Then name your future daughter after the phenomenal equal rights activist, Sojourner Truth – aka Belle (*c*.1797–1883).

A woman of mind-blowing bravery, Sojourner was born a slave but escaped with her daughter just ahead of the emancipation of slaves in New York State. When she discovered her son had been sold illegally to a family in Alabama, she took the case to court and totally smashed it. In a landmark victory, Sojourner won, freed her son and became the first black American ever to win a court case against a white person.

Sojourner went on to dedicate her life to leading a first-class campaign for anti-slavery laws, female equality and social justice. She toured across America delivered awe-inspiring speeches, empowering others to join the fight, and showed the world what can be achieved with a little bit of determination and big ol' dose of badassery.

BADASS RATING: ★★★★★
An iconic figure of strength and courage.

SOLOMON

Will your future son be blessed with wisdom? Then name him after one majorly judicious dude, King Solomon (d. *c.*931 BC).

Solomon reigned as the king of Israel for over forty years, during which time he earned himself the title of the wisest man in history for his sage advice and great leadership. Legend has it the guy could converse with birds, bats and any form of barnacle so he must have been pretty grade A+ on the wisdom scale.

He created the world's first ever holy temple, built in Jerusalem and constructed entirely of wood and gold in order to deliver maximum bling. He was a revered lyricist and poet, amazingly composing over 1,000 songs and 3,000 proverbs (or so they say). And somehow he still found time to serenade over 700 wives and 300 mistresses, as well as help anyone who turned up on his doorstep in need of some decent advice. This bro was busy.

BADASS RATING: ★★★★
Definitely lived his best life.

SOPHIA

Will your daughter be determined? Then name her after the princess, suffragette and socialite turned revolutionary, Sophia Duleep Singh (1876–1948).

Daughter of the last maharaja of the Sikh empire and the god-daughter of Queen Vic, Sophia was a fashion icon and darling of British society until she went on a trip to India, had an epiphany and returned to England with fire in her belly, and launched a mission to show the oppressive British government exactly who was boss.

Sophia threw herself into fighting for the suffragette cause. She embarrassed the Crown and enraged the state. Leader of the Black Friday march, she wrestled police officers to the ground, drove press carts across town, attacked politicians on the streets and was repeatedly arrested.

Sophia refused to pay taxes, refused to pay any fines for her behaviour and tore up her census papers declaring that women cannot vote and therefore do not count. Bold, brave and 100 per cent bona fide badass, Sophia put everything on the line to fight for freedom.

BADASS RATING: ★★★★★
The princess who brought down the patriarchy.

SOPHIE

Will your little girl be gutsy? Then name her after the badass teen rebel who stood up to the Nazis, Sophie Scholl (1921–43).

Along with her brother and some friends, Sophie founded the White Rose, a non-violent, fascist-fighting resistance group, during the Second World War. What started as a group of Munich University students determined to stand against the dictator became a movement across Germany. They distributed anti-Nazi and anti-war leaflets, launched an underground graffiti campaign across the country and stood against the system with immense bravery, courage and badassery. In 1943 the Gestapo caught Sophie and executed her for high treason. She was just twenty-one. After her death, millions of copies of the final leaflet, which had already been smuggled out of the country, were dropped by Allied forces across Germany.

BADASS RATING: ★ ★ ★ ★ ★
A symbol of hope and courage who dared to speak up.

Spartacus

Will your son lead an army of avengers against the world's biggest power? Yes? Then name him after the rebel slave who ignited the most furious revolt against the Roman Empire in history, Spartacus (*c.*111–71 BC).

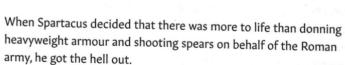

When Spartacus decided that there was more to life than donning heavyweight armour and shooting spears on behalf of the Roman army, he got the hell out.

Unfortunately, this led to his enslavement. He was shipped off to gladiatorial school to beat the shit out of other men in the name of light entertainment. Again he thought 'Stuff this', but this time he did things differently. He rallied seventy fellow gladiators, rinsed the school of all armour and weapons and bust out of the joint, destroying anyone who stood in the way.

Hiding out on Mount Vesuvius, Spartacus recruited more slaves. The Romans caught wind of this little rebellion and sent 3,000 soldiers to put an end to it. Assuming the rebel slaves would eventually run out of supplies and starve, they waited it out at the bottom of the mountain. Epic mistake.

Spartacus and his crew waited until moonlight and then abseiled down the cliff edge and destroyed the entire Roman squad like ninjas in the night. So 6,000 more soldiers were sent. And 6,000 soldiers died. By this point Spartacus had recruited over 70,000 slaves and they slayed and swindled their way through Roman towns and cities as part of the biggest uprising in history.

BADASS RATING: ★★★★★
A ballsy, brave and bodacious badass.

SUSAN

Will your future daughter have nerves of steel? Then name her after the daredevil French ambulance driver, Susan Travers (1909–2003).

During the Second World War, Susan worked for the French Foreign Legion, revving across minefields, swerving enemy attacks and transporting wounded soldiers to safety with ninja-like driving.

It was while stationed at the Free French fort, Bir Hakeim in Libya, that Susan came to deliver her most awe-inspiring act of badassery. In the boiling desert the unit found themselves surrounded by German forces. All women and helpers were ordered to leave, but Susan refused (partly because she was in love with the colonel – who also happened to be a White Russian prince – and partly because she was a total hardass, and no amount of German gunfire was going to make her sweat). So her fellow soldiers dug her a coffin-sized hole where she then hid for fifteen days in blistering hot temperatures, listening to the battle overhead.

With supplies dwindling, the French decided it was time to get out of there. In a daring midnight run, Susan jumped into the driver's seat of a nearby truck, blazed across the battlefield, open gunfire and led the 2,500 French troops through the pitch-black desert to safely.

BADASS RATING: ★★★★
A ballsy badass who makes Jeremy Clarkson look like a nervous pensioner behind the wheel of a Ford Focus.

SYBIL

Will your little progeny be born brave? Then name her after the teen who galloped across America on horseback to assemble the most hellraising militia in the history of the American Revolutionary War, Sybil Ludington (1761–1839).

In 1777 a spunky young Sybil, the oldest offspring of the Patriot Colonel Henry Ludington, mounted her horse and set off into the night on a mission to gather as many troops as possible to fight against British rule.

Riding like a bat out of hell, Sybil navigated her way through wild woodlands, persevered against torrential rain, outsmarted a murderous highwayman and covered more than 65 kilometres (40 miles) in a single evening. So effective was Sybil's war cry that by dawn over 400 warriors stood on the steps of her house, weapons raised and ready to kick British ass. Which of course they did.

BADASS RATING: ★★★
The sixteen-year-old rebel whose courageous journey helped liberate America.

MORE SMOKIN' Ss

SABLE

Sable Starr (1957–2009) was a flamboyant, free-living, free-loving wild child and 'queen of the groupies'.

BADASS RATING: ★★

SALVADOR

Salvador Dalí (1904–89) was the flamboyant, moustachioed, anti-authority surrealist artist who loved to be controversial.

BADASS RATING: ★

SAMUEL

Samuel White Baker (1821–93), an intrepid British explorer who spent his entire life chasing badass adventures across the globe, was famous for discovering a source of the river Nile.

BADASS RATING: ★★

MORE SMOKIN' Ss

SAPPHO

Sappho (*c*.620–*c*.570 BC), hailed as one of the greatest poets in existence by Plato, was the earliest known female writer and lyricist who unsurprisingly invented the Sapphic stanza.

BADASS RATING: ★ ★ ★ ★

SELMA

Selma James (b.1930), revered author, activist, feminist and all-round badass, founded the International Wages for Housework Campaign and started a global women's movement.

BADASS RATING: ★ ★ ★ ★

SELWYN

Selwyn Jepson (1899–1989) was the Second World War special agent who recruited hundreds of women into roles as undercover spies.

BADASS RATING: ★ ★

MORE SMOKIN' Ss

SHERWOOD

Sherwood Anderson (1876–1941) was an unconventional American novelist and artist.

BADASS RATING: ★★

SHULAMITH

Shulamith Firestone (1945–2012), writer, radical feminist and firebrand, started a second wave of feminism with the publication of her bestselling book, *The Dialectic of Sex*.

BADASS RATING: ★★★

STANISLAV

Stanislav Petrov (1939–2017) was the cool cucumber who singlehandedly saved the world from nuclear war.

BADASS RATING: ★★★★

MORE SMOKIN' Ss

STEDE

Stede Bonnet (1688–1718) was nicknamed 'The Gentleman Pirate' for his impeccable grooming and being the most stylish of all buccaneers.

BADASS RATING: ★★★

STELLA

Stella Benson (1892–1933), English writer, feminist and suffragette, was hailed as the unsung hero of the British literary canon. She was known for her humanity, wit and lifelong practice of diary writing.

BADASS RATING: ★★★

STEPHEN

Stephen King (b.1947) is simply the scariest writer of all time. Known as the 'King of Horror', this guy has bashed out some sixty novels that have even the bravest of readers cowering under the bed with some questionable stains on their pants.

BADASS RATING: ★★★★★

MORE SMOKIN' Ss

SYLVIA

Sylvia Pankhurst (1882–1960) was the revered patriarchy-smashing suffragette leader who also fought the fascists, capitalists and basically anyone who was being a dick.

BADASS RATING: ★★★★★

TALLULAH

Will your baby give the world the finger? Then name her after the wild, wisecracking queen of the stage and screen, Tallulah Bankhead (1902–68).

Outrageously witty, husky-voiced Tallulah Bankhead was a cartwheeling, underwear-shunning, Bentley-driving, ambisextrous badass from Alabama who had an electrifying acting career on both sides of the Atlantic. Tallulah shunned the conventional and yawnsome route of marriage and kids, instead feeding her all-consuming fever to be famous.

On a blazing path of badassery, she earned herself the title of one of the twentieth century's leading ladies of theatre, with a career spanning fifty years; she starred in fifty-one plays, eighteen films and infinite TV and radio performances.

Off screen, Tallulah spread her love with wild abandon. Famous for banging men and women and not giving a damn, she took roles based purely on the shaggability of the cast. Apparently she notched up a knock-out 500 conquests and even gave gonorrhoea the boot in an operation that nearly killed her. She also owned a pet lion named Winston Churchill. No biggie.

BADASS RATING: ★★★★
Fun-loving and fiercely cool; a champion of total excess.

TAMAR

Want to encourage your daughter to be sassy, strong and self-assured? Then name her after the regal powerhouse Queen Tamar (1166–1213).

Tamar ruled Georgia alongside her father from the age of twelve, honing her skills as a patriarchy-smashing, no-nonsense chick who much preferred to outsmart her enemies than draw a sword (although incidentally, when the need for her to draw her sword did arise – she totally kicked ass).

A few years later, old pops bit the dust and Tamar took sole power of the country. Quite a few of the men of Georgia were a little more than miffed about having a bird at the helm, so they tried to start a riot. With poise and grace and a big dose of badassery, Tamar quickly showed the rebels who was boss and chased them out of town. She replaced the old aristocratic government with savvy young officials hired purely on merit, and together they led Georgia to prosper.

When other countries invaded, Tamar casually batted them off like pesky summer flies. Anyone who tried to stage a coup was sent straight into exile, including her first husband, who had convinced himself that he could outsmart her. Not on your nelly, mate.

BADASS RATING: ★★★★
Georgia's first female ruler and badass of a saintly status – literally. The Orthodox Church canonized her as the Holy Righteous Queen.

Teddy

Is baby King of the Badasses? A corruption-smashing, rough-riding, peace-making, overachieving Oval Office resident, author, soldier, explorer and naturalist with so many badass qualities we need a whole new book to list them? Then name him Teddy after Teddy Roosevelt (1858–1919).

Crippled by severe asthma, Teddy was a man who could have lived quite comfortably on his inheritance. But did he? Did he hell. Elected as a state representative of New York at twenty-three (the youngest ever), he went on to become the youngest president of the United States, where he settled strikes, broke up powerful trusts and won a Nobel Peace Prize for negotiating the end of the Russo-Japanese War. He wrote eighteen books; he was a war hero, a cowboy, a mountain-climber and all-round king ass-whipper. A politician once said of his passing, 'Death had to take him sleeping, for if Roosevelt had been awake there would have been a fight.'

BADASS RATING: ★★★★★
A wunderkind, a king of badassery, this dude was a serious high flyer AND hard as nails.

TELESILLA

Will your little sprout be spunky, savvy and spirited? Then name her after the heroic Greek poet, Telesilla of Argos (*c.* fifth/sixth century BC).

A lyricist by day and a badass by night, Telesilla was a revered artist, knocking out Ancient Greek poetry at the rate that Marks & Spencer sells undercrackers (that's fast).

Around 570 BC, the Spartans decided to make a grab for the city of Argos, Telesilla's 'hood, and launched an attack. First they slayed the city's army. More warriors raced out, and they were killed too. The few men of Argos left clambered into the woods on the edge of the city and hid in trees. This wasn't the finest defence strategy. The Spartans easily found them, enticed them out from the shrubbery and chopped their heads off.

With no men left to defend the city, the Spartans were confident they had sealed the deal. But they had clearly underestimated the badassery of Telesilla. At midnight she went from house to house, rallying women and collecting utensils to use as weaponry. Girl gang assembled, Telesilla led them out to the enemy camp, ready to kick Spartan ass. As they approached, the Spartans grew anxious. Have their balls chopped off by a bunch of birds? What would the other Ancient Greek armies say? The risk to their reputation was too high: the Spartans fled. Argos was saved!

BADASS RATING: ★★★★
The writerly warrior who saved her city's ass.

THEODORA

Want to name your daughter after a sassy, sagacious empress who was also a bloody nice person and probably the most influential and powerful woman in Byzantine history? Then name her after Empress Theodora (*c*.497–548).

Theodora shimmied onto the stage at an early age to support her widowed mother. She rapidly became the star of the hippodrome: whether goading geese to peck grain from her groin or captivating crowds dancing in nothing but a carefully placed ribbon, teenage Theodora owned it.

At twenty-one she met Justinian I. He was so enchanted by her awesomeness that he repealed a law prohibiting high military officials from marrying actors, so that he could wed her. His mother violently disapproved, but Theodora gave not a monkey's as she skipped down the aisle to become empress.

A badass champion of women and their rights, Empress Theodora instituted the death penalty for rape, passed laws prohibiting forced prostitution, culled brothels and created convents for ex-prostitutes. She forbade killings of adulterous women, gave mothers guardianship rights over their children and fought to banish sexual slavery.

Theodora kicked political corruption to the kerb. During the Nika Riots she famously thrust past the convention of 'No women talking during council' and charged in, declaring that her husband and his crew should live and die by their city, not run into hiding like scared mice! So they did. And Empress Theodora is credited in history for saving her husband's throne (and ass).

BADASS RATING: ★★★★★
The most influential and bitchin' empress of all time!

THOMAS

Want to inspire your future son to work hard and achieve greatness? Then name him after the sweaty American inventor, Thomas Alva Edison (1847–1931).

Thomas spent his life avoiding sleep and creating an abundance of useful things. His endless experimentation and perseverance gave the world electric generators, batteries, the microphone, tattoo guns and the phonograph. Ensuring no time was ever wasted, he once accidentally blew up a train carriage with an unruly chemistry experiment he was conducting in transit. He got a lifetime travel ban. We got the light bulb.

BADASS RATING: ★ ★ ★ ★ ★
The guy had over 2,000 patents worldwide. What have you done with your life?

THOREAU

Want to inspire your son to enjoy the beauty of the natural world? Then name him after the writer and philosopher who sought a self-sufficient life in tune with nature, Henry David Thoreau (1817–62).

The guy who gave brain boners to a heap of twentieth-century civil rights leaders, Thoreau was an American transcendentalist and hailed a great anarchist for his anti-establishment philosophy. He courageously expressed his disgust for the institution of slavery and spoke against the American war in Mexico. Famous for writing the essay *Resistance to Civil Government*, Thoreau's ideas later inspired both Gandhi and Martin Luther King.

A man of simple living, Thoreau escaped to the wilderness in a bid to gain more understanding of humanity. After his time among the trees, he vowed to return to the city but live free from the shackles of society.

BADASS RATING: ★ ★ ★
A radical political activist and spiritual visionary.

Tobias

Is it written in the stars that your future child will become a maths marvel? Then name him after the master of eighteenth-century moon-mapping, self-taught mathematician and genius, Tobias Mayer (1723–62).

Tobias had a brain so almighty that, despite a very basic schooling, by the age of eighteen this numbers whizz-kid had published several books on geometry and made a decent living spreading his love of maths through teaching. Snapped up to work with a renowned cartographic establishment in his twenties, Tobias took one long look at the map-making industry, drew a deep sigh and set about making some serious improvements to its method, gaining him a banging reputation in the world of science. From mapping the earth to mapping the moon: it was during his post at the University of Göttingen that Tobias began the work that created his legacy. While other astronomers were squabbling over the need for a new lunar model, Tobias, ever the maverick, simply made more accurate observations and then more accurate calculations than those around him, publishing the first-rate lunar tables that earned him a place in history.

BADASS RATING: ★★

A mathematical autodidact who went on to become one of the leading astronomers of the eighteenth century.

TOMOE

Will your little cub grow up to be strong and valorous? Name her after Tomoe Gozen (1157–1247), a sword-spinning, arrow-shooting, head-slicing warrior and the most legendary female samurai that ever lived.

Tomoe was a kickass archer and swordswoman and commanded horses with superb skill, riding down treacherous paths that others feared to take. She couldn't care less that she was female and supposed to use a weapon reserved only for women; instead she fought with a katana, a sword normally used in combat by male samurai. And boy, did she show them how to use it.

Tomoe might have been the lover of warlord Minamoto no Yoshinaka, but she was also the fierce leader of his army. She won battles against enemies of over 6,000 with a casual 300 samurai. She fought hundreds of attackers off sacred soil with just one sword. When an enemy general named Uchida Ieyoshi attempted to capture her by pulling her from her horse, Tomoe sliced off his wayward hand, charged at him with brutal skill, decapitated him and then rode the battle line with his head as a trophy, swinging proudly in the wind.

BADASS RATING: ★★★★★
Tomoe kicked samurai ass like a boss.

Toussaint

Will your future son be brave, bold and with badassery in abundance? Then name him after the anti-colonization, anti-slavery crusader who victoriously led the most legendary slave revolt in history, Toussaint L'Ouverture (1743–1803).

Born into slavery in the country now known as Haiti, Toussaint defied colonial powers by learning to read and write, practising a considerable amount of pyromania and pumping a shitload of iron to ensure his guns were made up of 100 per cent steel.

Allegedly calling on the powers of the Vodou gods to guide him on his trailblazing mission, in 1791 Toussaint assembled an army of beefcakes and led one of the biggest, bloodiest and most successful acts of self-liberation in history. Buildings were burnt, plantations were ravaged and families cursed as rebellion spread across the island. The rebels triumphed and the abolition of slavery ensued.

A free man, Toussaint rose to power, appointed himself Governor General for Life of his country and rebranded it Haiti. He then tirelessly defeated French, Spanish and British invaders and did a heap of cool things to boost the island's economy and cultural legacy.

BADASS RATING: ★★★★★
The revolutionary who drove the most badass slave revolt in history and paved the way for Haiti's independence from colonial rule.

TOVE

Want your little Snorkmaiden to share her moniker with the strong-willed, multitalented, fascist-fighting Finnish artist, writer and inventor of the lovable, imperfect and extraordinary Moomins? Then name her Tove, after Tove Marika Jansson (1914–2001).

The princes and princesses in children's literature could kiss Moomin ass: here at last was someone with the balls to birth characters who got intoxicated on palm wine, smoked tobacco, swore, misbehaved and loved whomever they damn well wanted to. Tove famously called out Hitler for being a whining toddler in the throes of an almighty, red-hot tantrum in her cartoons for Swedish journal *Garm* during the Second World War. She objected to archaic Finnish policies and she didn't give two ticks that homosexuality was illegal in Finland. While Thingummy and Bob may have talked in secret in the Moomin books, Tove championed love without boundaries.

BADASS RATING: ★★★
Tove batted off Walt Disney's advances and remained an unapologetic, extremely talented artist and all-round badass.

TRUDI

Will your daughter be dauntless, determined and ready to make a splash? Then name her after 'Queen of the Waves', champion athlete, gold medallist and first woman to swim across the English Channel, Gertrude Ederle (1905–2003).

On 6 August 1926, Trudi donned a two-piece bathing suit and a pair of goggles, then coated herself in grease before wading out into the freezing cold waters of the Cap Gris-Nez. Wanting to prove that women were just as capable as men of competing in dangerous and difficult swimming challenges, she begin to swim the infamous stretch of sea between France and England. She dodged jellyfish, persevered through violent storms and pushed against strong currents. Powered by sugar cubes and a large dose of badassery, Trudi swam 56 kilometres (35 miles), finally reaching the English coast in just fourteen hours and thirty-one minutes, beating the times of all of the men who had swum before her.

BADASS RATING: ★★★★★
The ballsy badass who proved that women can do absolutely anything.

TURA

Is your baby kicking so hard that it feels like a kung fu master assaulting your diaphragm? Then name her after the fierce and fearless, Tura Satana (1938–2011).

Tura was raped by a group of teenagers when she was ten, but her attackers were never prosecuted. Hearing rumours the judge had been paid off, Tura refused to sit about taking this kind of shit so she trained in martial arts, earned her black belt and set out to exact revenge on her rapists, serving her own form of justice with a jaw-breaking karate chop. Hell-bent on protecting others, she formed a girl gang that prowled the mean streets of Chicago. When her parents tried to tame her by forcing her into an arranged marriage, she quickly left for Los Angeles.

From burlesque dancer to star of the screen, Tura blazed across Hollywood leaving a trail of badassery in her wake. She famously taught Elvis how to dance. She also crushed balls (and necks) in various action films, performing her own stunts and gaining even more badass points for her role of Varla (also a great name) in the legendary *Faster Pussycat, Kill Kill!* – a film that would later inspire Quentin Tarantino to write *Kill Bill*.

BADASS RATING: ★★★★★
Actor and total hardass. All hail Tura!

Tycho

Will your little fawn be a freewheeling and fearless future scientist? Then name him after the data geek and astronomy pioneer, Tycho Brahe (1546–1601).

Tycho had all the right qualities to be the ultimate mad scientist – first-class facial hair, a cosmic-sized brain and a bonkers family. He was all set for law school until he witnessed a solar eclipse at the age of fifteen. During the momentary darkness, Tycho experienced his own personal solar flare and so began his career as a ground-breaking, gold-nosed astronomer whose planetary predictions have become as legendary as his perpetual partying.

He was the sort of bloke who liked to settle his astronomical altercations with fellow scholars by sword. On one particular occasion he lost not only the argument but also most of his nose. To fix his newly created facial black hole, he simply glued a chunk of solid gold in its place.

Remembered for cataloguing shitloads of stars (over 1,000) and being the first to identify planetary motion, Tycho was a pretty big deal in his day. The king of Denmark was so in awe he gifted him his own island, where Tycho then built the most pimping observatory-cum-party palace, complete with its own entertainment – a clairvoyant dwarf named Jepp, a pet elk who liked to drink beer and a dungeon full of madcap inventions.

BADASS RATING: ★★★★
Stellar scientist and badass.

MORE TERRIBLE Ts

TAKSIN

Taksin the Great (1734–82) was a guerrilla fighter turned king who liberated Thailand from Burmese rule by forming an army of rebel soldiers who blasted enemy troops.

BADASS RATING: ★★★★

TATYANA

Tatyana Fazlalizadeh (b.1985), mega-skilled American artist and activist, was famous for sticking up for every woman who has ever been accosted by a stranger with the words, 'Cheer up, love, it might never happen.'

BADASS RATING: ★★★★

TAVI

Tavi Gevinson (b.1996) is the accidental teen fashion prodigy who started a casual blog on clothes from her bedroom aged eleven, and became a star.

BADASS RATING: ★★★★

MORE TERRIBLE Ts

TERESA

Teresa Magbanua (1868–1947), hailed as the Joan of Arc of the Visayas, was the fearless Filipina warrior who led soldiers in the Visayas and kicked both American and Spanish ass.

BADASS RATING: ★★★★

THADDEUS

Thaddeus Stevens (1792–1868) was a civil rights campaigner and radical politician who fought for the emancipation of slaves in America.

BADASS RATING: ★★★★★

THELONIOUS

Thelonious Sphere Monk (1917–82) was an experimental jazz artist and composer.

BADASS RATING: ★★★★

MORE TERRIBLE Ts

THEODOROS

Theodoros Kolokotronis (1770–1844) was a Greek rebel general who beat the shit out of the Ottoman Empire and liberated Greece.

BADASS RATING: ★ ★ ★ ★

THOR

Thor Heyerdahl (1914–2002), an intrepid Norwegian adventurer, built a boat using only balsawood, bamboo and hemp and then sailed over 5,000 miles across choppy waters in his homemade raft.

BADASS RATING: ★ ★ ★ ★

TIBERIUS

Emperor Tiberius Caesar (42 BC–37 AD) was a toga-sporting, riotous and rebellious ruler of the Roman Empire.

BADASS RATING: ★ ★ ★

MORE TERRIBLE Ts

TRUMAN

Truman Henry Safford (1836–1901) was the numbers whizz who could answer mind-boggling maths questions via turbo-charged mental arithmetic.

BADASS RATING: ★★★★

URRACA

Will your newest hatchling rule the roost? Will she show her brothers and sisters that she is the boss? Yes? Then name her after the Spanish countess who inherited a city, warded off various attacks and generally kicked everyone's ass, Urraca of Zamora (*c.*1033–1101).

As Urraca's father, Ferdinand I the Great, lay on his deathbed, he divvied up his empire and gave each of his five children a walled city or small kingdom to call their own. Urraca inherited Zamora, and she ruled with kindness and generosity. Her older bruv, however, was less than pleased that he wasn't left the whole of papa's empire, and set about wrangling what he deemed rightly his back from his other siblings. But when he came to attack Urraca's city, he found he had messed with the wrong sister.

Urraca raised her defences so that her brother's army was unable to advance on the city's walls. She then grabbed the nearest spear-carrying Spaniard who looked like he could spin a good yarn and sent him on a mission that would save Zamora. The man pledged his allegiance to her brother's army and wormed his way into their camp. Then, once it looked like he was best of buds with Urraca's brother, he pulled out his spear and killed him.

BADASS RATING: ★ ★ ★
Fought back like a boss.

URSULA

Will your future daughter be daring and dauntless? Then name her after the feisty and fearless Soviet spy, Ursula Kuczynski (1907–2000).

One of the longest-serving spies, Ursula's espionage career began in Shanghai when she was just twenty-three. Under the guise of a bookseller and then housewife, Ursula gathered vital intelligence for the Soviet Union – first in China, then Switzerland, before moving to work undercover in Britain.

Ursula built and installed a DIY radio transmitter in her house in Oxfordshire and, alongside Klaus Fuchs, relayed nuclear secrets back to the Russians with insane confidence. No one would suspect a kind-natured mother of three to be quietly engaged in the most dangerous of espionage activities.

As suspicion grew over Klaus's involvement with the Russians, Ursula decided it was time to get the hell outta there and fled back to her homeland of Germany, where she casually reinvented herself as a successful children's book writer.

BADASS RATING: ★★★★
One of the greatest female secret agents of the last century.

ANOTHER UBER/UNIQUE U

ULPIA

Ulpia Severina (*c.* third century AD) was the feisty and formidable first and only female ruler of the classical Roman Empire.

BADASS RATING: ★★★★

VALENTINA

Will your little rocket blaze a trail across the stars? Then name her after the first female cosmonaut to fly to space, Valentina Tereshkova (b.1937).

Russian-born Valentina was working on the production line in a textile factory, falling out of planes for funsies as an amateur sky-diver and dreaming of adventure when she was selected out of thousands of applicants to join the Soviet space programme.

Undergoing a gruelling training regime that included over a hundred free falls, sweltering in full flight gear in a thermal chamber at over 80 degrees Celsius, enduring solitary confinement, endless interrogation on all aspects of spacecraft engineering and being relentlessly flung arse over tit, Valentina prepared to take on space.

In June 1963, she made history as the first woman to blast off into space. On board the Vostok 6 in a landmark mission that lasted almost three days, Valentina orbited the earth a casual forty-eight times and covered a whopping 1.97 million kilometres. She made jokes, survived a near-fatal computer malfunction (which she managed to manually reset, despite suffering from extreme nausea and concussion), and clocked up more hours in space than the combined time of all American astronauts who had flown before her. Respect.

BADASS RATING: ★★★★★
A stellar astronaut and human being, and still the only woman ever to have completed a solo space voyage.

VELVALEE

Want to name your little bundle after a woman considered by some as the Second World War's most unlikely and devious spy? Then take inspiration from Velvalee Malvena Dickinson (1893–1980).

Velvalee was a smart American chick who merrily involved herself in some pretty sassy, high-profile espionage activity.

Velvalee adored Japan and its culture and alongside her husband, she joined the Japanese-American Society, throwing splendid dinner parties for numerous visiting members of the Japanese military and government. After moving to New York, Velvalee opened an antique dolls shop on Madison Avenue. For a business that could barely cover its overheads, she had a lavish amount of money; some sharp people might have asked where it was all coming from? The answer was the Japanese.

Velvalee may have looked like a mousey little woman with large thick-rimmed spectacles, running a quaint little shop on the Upper East Side, but she was in fact a cunning spy reporting to the Japanese on the position and activities of the United States navy. Using the language of dolls, Velvalee was able to report the positions of the US military, with emphasis on the state of repair of vessels at Pearl Harbor.

Eventually, her letters were intercepted by the FBI, and Velvalee was hauled from her shop into a street of eager bystanders, then charged with espionage and violation of wartime censorship codes.

Agents found over $15,000 stashed in her safe deposit box. Velvalee protested that her then-dead husband was in fact the spy, before surrendering and begging for mercy.

BADASS RATING: ★★
Velvalee managed to bust out of prison after ten years, but history will forever remember her as the badass spy known as 'Doll Woman'.

VENUS

Will your little supremo be born with athletic prowess? Will she dream big and deliver record-breaking tennis serves? Take inspiration from one of the greatest female players in the world and four-time Olympic gold medallist, Venus Ebony Starr Williams (b.1980).

Venus started playing tennis at three years old and by ten, she had already shown the world she could ace a serve of over 160 kilometres per hour. By the time she was fourteen, she was playing tennis as a pro, beating top fifty-ranked whizz Shaun Stafford in her first professional game. By the age of twenty, she had won gold in the women's singles at the Sydney Olympic Games, and smashed her way to another gold playing with her sister in the doubles tournament the same year.

BADASS RATING: ★★★★
The first black woman ever to be ranked world number one by the Women's Tennis Association.

VERA

Is your future daughter a born leader? Will she be daring and dauntless to boot? Then name her after the brains and balls behind the Second World War's biggest spy network, Vera Atkins (1908–2000).

During the Second World War, Vera worked for the Special Operations Executive, helping to lead a network of over 500 British spies working in German-occupied France. In between smuggling vital war information back to Churchill, kicking Nazi ass and charming the pants off the enemy with such skill and class that she could extract the most confidential German intelligence, Vera also recruited and trained fellow secret agents. She liaised with their families, helped create impeccable cover stories and relentlessly risked her life to hunt down those who went missing.

Vera also negotiated with Nazi intelligence, evaded all Gestapo attempts on her life and, with the words of Churchill ringing in her ears, she quite literally 'set Europe ablaze' in the fight for freedom.

BADASS RATING: ★★★★★
The boss behind Churchill's secret army.

VICTORIA

Will your little one grow up to conquer the world? Then name her after the patriarchy-smashing powerhouse who dared to be different, Victoria Woodhull (1838–1927).

Victoria's childhood was spent touring the country with her sister, communicating with the dead and healing the sick. But she left all this behind when she managed to free herself from the confines of her abusive father to become a mega-successful businesswoman, politician and activist.

Victoria set up the very first female-run newspaper in the United States, a voice on women's suffrage, free love and lots of other controversial topics, including outing various misogynists in the nineteenth-century version of the #TimesUp campaign. That same year she also set up the very first female-owned brokerage company on Wall Street, made a tonne of money, gave most of her wealth to charity and then used the rest to run for president.

Yep, at thirty-four, Victoria ran for US president. Before women had even won the right to vote, this high-flying sister was making a charge for the Oval Office.

AUTHOR'S NOTE – if the name Victoria is a little too traditional, why not take inspiration from the monikers she chose for her own children – Byron and Zulu?

BADASS RATING: ★★★★
A bewitching businesswoman and boundary-busting badass.

Violette

Will your daughter be vibrant and valorous? Then name her after the Second World War secret agent, Violette Szabo (1921–45).

When Violette's husband was killed in battle, she decided it was time to up her game in the war effort and applied to work for the British Special Operations Executive. She was calm, confident, a crack shot and had guns of steel; she was fluent in French and English and the language of badassery – basically the perfect spy.

Her first assignment saw her drop down into France, assume a false identity and wreak total havoc. She started riots in German base camps, sabotaged their industrial plants and left a trail of destruction in her wake. When she discovered that the Nazis were holding over a hundred French Resistance workers hostage, she instigated a rescue mission.

Her second assignment began just after the D-Day landings and was just as dangerous as the first. When her car hit a German roadblock midway through the operation, Violette judo-kicked her way out of the passenger's side, gun in hand, blasted the Nazis and escaped to some nearby woods. Although the Gestapo eventually caught up with her, Violette was one of the most daring, heroic and hellraising spies in British history.

BADASS RATING: ★★★★
The Nazi-slaying secret who gave her life in the fight for freedom during the Second World War.

VIRGINIA

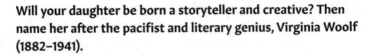

Will your daughter be born a storyteller and creative? Then name her after the pacifist and literary genius, Virginia Woolf (1882–1941).

Described as fierce, energetic and humorous, Virginia was experimental – a writerly rebel, and a pioneer in feminist writing. During her lifetime she penned nine novels, three biographies, countless short stories, essays and works of non-fiction exploring art, history, politics and sexism. Her immense creative spirit has inspired generations, and her landmark publication, *A Room of One's Own*, is one of the most iconic feminist texts today.

BADASS RATING: ★★★★
A symbol of female liberation.

VIVIENNE

Want to inspire your little rebel to lead a style revolution? Want her to embrace the original and the outrageous? Of course you do. Name her after the queen of punk and coolest damn designer to have ever walked this planet, Vivienne Westwood (b.1941).

Subversive, smart and sassy, Vivienne grew up on a council estate in Cheshire before moving to London to study at art school. She started out working as a primary school teacher and making jewellery in the evenings to sell at Portobello Market. From modest beginnings to becoming Britain's most iconic designer, Vivienne has always dared to break the mould. Hailed with co-inventing punk as well as revolutionizing design, she is a controversial genius.

An eco-warrior and human rights activist, Vivienne is not afraid to provoke, protest or proclaim her support for the causes she believes in or give two fingers to the establishment. She once dressed up as Margaret Thatcher on the front cover of *Tatler*; she gave male models boobs on the catwalk; and in support of vegetarianism she thought nothing of stripping naked for a PETA video (that's People for the Ethical Treatment of Animals). She also protested against anti-terror laws by creating iconic T-shirts declaring 'I AM NOT A TERRORIST, please don't arrest me', and once drove up to David Cameron's house in a tank.

BADASS RATING: ★★★★
A maverick, a machine and an almighty legend.

MORE VALIANT Vs

VALERIE

Valerie Solanas (1936–88), writer, radical feminist and bat-shit crazy activist, founded the Society for Cutting Up Men and then tried to kill Andy Warhol.

BADASS RATING: ★

VINCENZO

Vincenzo Peruggia (1881–1925) was a daring dissident of Italian origin who had such brazen badassery he only went and stole the bloody *Mona Lisa*.

BADASS RATING: ★★

WALLACE

Will your wee bairn be born to lead a fearsome quest for independence? Yes? Then name him after the claymore-wielding, tartan-clad, Buckfast-drinking thirteenth-century Scottish warrior, William Wallace (*c.*1270–1305).

Wallace spearheaded the rebellion against English rule in Scotland under King Edward I. What started as an act of revenge grew to a full-scale revolt, with Scottish rebels charging across the border, raiding towns and generally making mincemeat out of the English army.

It all began when the English sheriff of Lanark Castle brutally murdered Wallace's wife. Little did he know he'd messed with the wrong man. Wallace assembled a group of rebels (probably with a rallying cry along the lines of, 'They can have our lives but they will never take our freedom!') and then promptly killed the sheriff.

As unrest in Scotland grew, more warriors joined Wallace and he drove the English out of every corner of Scotland. Leading a fierce army of kilt-wearing reprobates, Wallace famously won the Battle of Stirling Bridge in 1297. Against all odds, 8,000 Scots kicked the shit out of 50,0000 English soldiers in a landmark victory that saw Wallace knighted as the Guardian of Scotland.

Wallace continued to demonstrate the colossal size of his balls and generally wreak havoc for the English until his execution in 1305, whereupon Scottish rebels persisted with the fight and eventually triumphed, gaining complete independence.

BADASS RATING: ★★★★★
The beloved Scottish hero and savage freedom fighter who guided his country to independence.

WALTER

Will your future son be a crack shot? Then name him after the gangster-slaying FBI agent turned Olympic marksman, Walter Walsh (1907–2014).

From a young age, Walter could hit a bull's eye. He could shoot apples clean in half, lit cigarettes from the mouths of his companions, balls flying through the air and just about anything that moved.

After winning a bunch of trophies in amateur sharpshooting competitions at university, he joined the FBI and got paid to roam the streets of America with a Magnum .375 tucked into his jacket. In no time, Walter had become one of the FBI's top agents. He led death-defying shootouts, went undercover and took down a heap of notorious American gangsters, including the infamous mafia boss Doc Barker, and relentlessly risked his life on various secret missions that made it look like James Bond had it easy.

Once Walter had finished enforcing justice on the outlaws of America, he entered the Olympic Games and other worldwide championships for people who like to shoot shit and, of course, took home gold.

BADASS RATING: ★★
Definitely someone you wouldn't want to get on the wrong side of.

WOLF

Will your future son be built like a brick? Then name him after one of the most successful Irish kings in history, Wolf the Quarrelsome (*c*.900c–*c*.1000).

The younger bruv of Brian Boru, Wolf was known for being a towering, hard-as-nails, nuts, revenge-seeking, long-axe-wielding, Viking-slaying, ass-kicking giant, as you would frankly expect of a man they called Wolf the Quarrelsome.

He is known for beating the horns out of the Viking army in the Battle of Clontarf, a victory that freed the Irish from the greedy clutches of the horn helmet-clad Nords, and which established Brian Boru as an Irish national hero. When the king was later killed by Brodir, leader of the Viking army, Wolf immediately hunted him down, sliced open his abdomen and chased him round and round the trunk of a tree, and 'so wound all his entrails out of him', before leaving him to die in one of history's most brutal revenge killings. Don't mess with Wolf.

BADASS RATING: ★★★★
Lauded as the greatest warrior of eleventh-century Ireland, Wolf was a bull-headed brute hell-bent on eradicating Viking rule.

WU

Will your daughter rule the world? Then name her after the only female emperor in Chinese history, Wu Zetian (624–705).

Historians have given Wu a bad rep for being a power-hungry, ruthless and murderous empress. The story of her rise goes something like this: Wu shacks up with Emperor Taizong. He dies and his son comes to power, so Wu starts mating with him. They sprout a few sprogs. Hungry and hell-bent on controlling China, Wu slyly arranges the deaths of each member of the ruling family (including her own children) that lies in her path to domination. In 690 Wu reigns. It is quite possible most of this is not true.

In fact, during her time as empress, Wu made great waves in terms of the advancement of women's rights. She gave women equal status. She hired a female prime minister, enabled women to own land and ordered numerous biographers to document the stories of strong Chinese women. Wu also hired government and education officials on merit, rather than class or gender, and during her rule elevated China to superpower status.

It is therefore pretty suspicious that history has been so unkind to an empress who was good at her job and pro-women and pro-equality. The story of her rise to power is even more dubious given she then abdicated the throne to her son. But wherever the truth lies, no one can argue that Wu was one helluva leader.

BADASS RATING: ★★★
The ultimate boss lady.

MORE WICKED Ws

WANGARI

Wangari Maathai (1940–2011), an awe-inspiring eco-warrior and women's rights activist, was the first African woman to receive the Nobel Peace Prize.

BADASS RATING: ★★★★★

WENDELL

Wendell Phillips (1811–84) was the oppression-slaying abolitionist and lawyer who dedicated his life to ending slavery and racial and gender inequality.

BADASS RATING: ★★★★

WILFRED

Wilfred Owen (1893–1918) was the treasured British troubadour whose lyrical account of the front line during the First World War represents some of the most badass and brave poetry on planet earth.

BADASS RATING: ★★★★

MORE WICKED Ws

WILLA

Willa Brown (1906–92), an awe-inspiring aviator, was the first African-American woman to earn her pilot's licence in the United States and run for Congress.

BADASS RATING: ★★★★

WINIFRED

Winifred Davidson (b. *c.*1920) was a daring Canadian spy who worked as part of Britain's Special Operations Executive during the Second World War.

BADASS RATING: ★★★

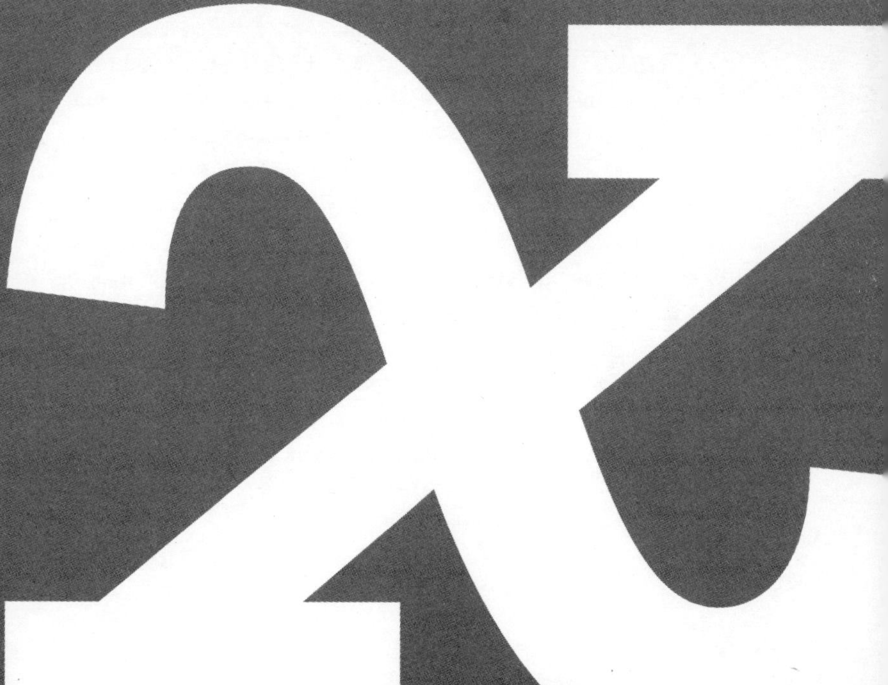

XAVIER

Will your little tiddler become a master skier? Will he glide across mountains and power down black runs in the pursuit of extreme adventure? Then name him after the Swiss ski champion and intrepid explorer, Xavier Mertz (1882–1913).

Built like a brick shithouse and with zero sense of danger, Xavier was used to jumping from insane heights, traversing crevasse-strewn mountains, scaling 1,000-metre cliffs* and generally defying death and common sense in equal measure.

In 1911, along with some other equally hardcore adventurers and a pack of huskies, Xavier set off on a mission to conquer the unconquerable – the South Pole. In sub-zero temperatures, and enduring raging winds, blizzards, storms and just about every extreme Mother Nature could throw his way, Xavier powered across the Antarctic on a pair of skis, heading for deep wilderness. On day thirty-five, disaster struck when a member of his crew fell down a crevasse, taking all the food supplies with him. This was a tad inconvenient. Forced to abort the mission, Xavier did a U-turn back to base camp. Despite being an A1 badass, even Xavier could not survive thirty-five days without food and water and he pegged out at some point on the journey home; but he is forever remembered as one of the most fearless adventurers of all time.

* This might not be 100 per cent true.

BADASS RATING: ★★★
The rugged mountaineer and ski supremo who tried to conquer the South Pole.

YAA

Will your little lioness be brave, bold and bodacious? Then give her the name of the courageous African queen who led a war against colonial rule, Yaa Asantewaa (1840–1921).

In the late nineteenth century, things were not looking great for the people of Ashanti. The British Empire had set up camp in their palace and was out to gain complete control of their confederacy. Yaa's grandson, the king of Ashanti, had been shipped off to Sierra Leone and held hostage with a bunch of other Ashanti chiefs; and after years of war and unrest, everyone was at breaking point. On top of this, some British governor was demanding ownership of the most sacred symbol of the Ashanti people, the Golden Stool.

Just as the Ashanti officials were about to completely surrender, up stood Yaa. Delivering a speech off the scale in badassitude, Yaa empowered her people by saying something along the lines of, 'Don't sit back and take this shit, you cowards.' Then she suggested that the men who weren't prepared to fight might want to swap their loincloths for her panties, and with that she fired a single bullet. And so began one of the greatest rebellions against British rule.

Assembling and leading an army of 5,000, Yaa sieged British forts, seized supplies, built stockades, sliced off a few heads here and there and power-marched across battlefields like a boss.

A revered hero in what is now modern-day Ghana, Yaa is a symbol of resistance, courage and extreme badassery.

BADASS RATING: ★★★★
The silver-haired warrior queen who kicked colonial ass.

MORE YOKELISH Ys

YASMEEN

Yasmeen Lari (b.1942) was a social justice activist and architect who set up a humanitarian organization that helped build houses in poor areas across the world in the aftermath of war and natural disaster.

BADASS RATING: ★ ★ ★ ★

YEAGER

Chuck Yeager (b.1923), American pilot and speed-demon, smashed records by becoming the first person to travel faster than the speed of sound, doing so with a couple of broken ribs from a horseriding accident the day before.

BADASS RATING: ★ ★ ★ ★ ★

YNES

Ynes Mexia (1870–1938) was the plant-loving, ground-breaking adventurer who scaled rock faces, hid in the depths of the Amazon and fought off poisonous snakes in the name of discovery.

BADASS RATING: ★ ★ ★

ZAPPA

Want to encourage your little virtuoso to be unique? Then name him after the musical maverick and swaggering rock iconoclast who relentlessly broke the artistic mould, Frank Zappa (1940–93).

Zappa stormed onto the scene with The Mothers of Invention, a band that rebelled against everything pop music was synonymous with. Purveyor of the weird and sporting the finest handlebar moustache on the Sunset Strip, Zappa shook up the music world with his controversial compositions, satirical lyrics and phenomenal talent. From pop and soul, jazz and acid rock, nu-metal, electronic to orchestral, Zappa played it, mixed it and in his own words 'extrapolated it to the extreme'.

He took zero shit from industry bruisers, shunned the mainstream, sued the corporates (and won); he funded his own tours, payrolled his musicians, built his own damn recording studio and record company – he was basically a rare-breed musical maestro of the 100 per cent organic variety, a free-range rock 'n' roller who had complete artistic control. With over eighty albums to his name, Zappa was without doubt one of the most ground-breaking musicians of all time.

BADASS RATING: ★★★★
A musical anarchist and pure legend.

ZAZEL

Did your little daredevil launch herself into the world in spectacular style? Then name her after the death-defying acrobat who introduced the most explosive finale to her circus act, Zazel Rossa Matilda Richter (1863–1937).

Zazel was already a daring trapeze artist, wowing audiences with her breathtaking stunts, dancing along high-wire ropes, performing the flying trapeze and generally pulling off tricks with insane amounts of badassitude.

Then in April 1877, she debuted a new act – the human cannonball. Thanks to some large coiled springs expertly placed at the bottom of a long metal barrel, Zazel momentarily waved her audience goodbye before being propelled 20 metres into the air. Her flight path was quite unpredictable, and during each performance Zazel would plaster on a dazzling smile while secretly praying to the Lord, Jesus, Holy Mary and Mother of God that she would land somewhere within the vicinity of the safety net.

The act was an instant success and drew crowds in the thousands, until one day the high-risk business of blasting a small human out of a giant metal cannon went awry. Thankfully Zazel only broke her spine in about eight places, but after that she decided it was time to retire.

BADASS RATING: ★★★★
The world's first ever human cannonball.

ZELDA

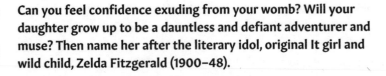

Can you feel confidence exuding from your womb? Will your daughter grow up to be a dauntless and defiant adventurer and muse? Then name her after the literary idol, original It girl and wild child, Zelda Fitzgerald (1900–48).

Born into a middle-class Alabaman family, Zelda gave patriarchy the fist and spent her teenage years drinking, dancing, partying hard and doing as she pleased. She shrugged off the expectations of 'how a woman should behave' and joined in with whatever the boys in her town did, and why not?

Men and women adored her. Elusive and flirtatious, she eventually accepted novelist Scott Fitzgerald's proposal (but only after his first book deal), and refused to succumb to the life of a housewife.

Unafraid to dance on tabletops, dive naked into fountains, roar up and down the streets of New York atop a taxi cab with the wind blowing feverishly through her hair, or get thrown out of hotel after hotel for her hedonistic behaviour, Zelda chose to live life like it was one long badass party, without a single care in the world.

Her writing made it into her husband's works, possibly more than was ever acknowledged, and she published a novel of her own, penned in haste in a mere six weeks just to kick ass. Zelda grabbed the bull of life by the horns and LIVED it.

BADASS RATING: ★★★★★
An icon of the jazz age with an infectious zest for life.

ZENO

Will your future son flourish in the after-school debate club? Then name him after the Greek philosopher, Zeno of Elea (*c.*490–*c.*430 BC).

Zeno was seriously good at winning arguments by employing a kickass combination of logic and reason. He also had a talent for inventing paradoxes, creating the famous one involving a race between Achilles and a tortoise. When he wasn't thinking deep thoughts and questioning the meaning of life, Zeno was part of a band of renegade rebels who assembled to bring down the tyrant ruler known as Nearchus.

While Zeno may have been damn good at claiming victory in philosophical debate, he was less successful when staging a coup. He was caught, arrested and then tortured in a bid to make him reveal the rest of his crew of conspirators. But Zeno refused to surrender the names, instead suggesting that he knew a secret that would be advantageous to Nearchus. As Nearchus got close enough to hear what it was, Zeno bit off his ear.

BADASS RATING: ★★
A sage scholar with the gift of the gab.

ZENOBIA

Will your little princess rise up and start a riot? Yes? Then name her after the warrior queen who told the Romans where to stick their empire, Zenobia (240–274 AD).

When her eldest son was killed and her other son too young to rule, Zenobia came to reign over the Roman colony of Palmyra. She supposedly had various duties to the Roman Empire, but she sacked that off and led a famous revolt against them instead. First she conquered Egypt, then she forcefully expanded her territory to the countries now known as Turkey and Syria. By this point the Romans had noticed a fairly large-scale rebellion charging across the horizon, but Zenobia was on an unstoppable mission. She cut off trading supplies to Rome, started wars with Lebanon and Palestine and generally showed Emperor Aurelian just how easy it was to kick his ass.

BADASS RATING: ★★★★
Warrior. Queen. Badass who almost brought the Roman Empire to an end.

MORE ZANY Zs

ZENA

Zena Dare (1887–1975) was the whip-smart, waggish and wondrous British actor who went from child star to revered siren of the stage and screen in a career that spanned six decades.

BADASS RATING: ★★

ZEPHANIAH

Zephaniah Williams (1795–1874) was a freethinking Welsh coal miner who led one of the greatest rebellions in British history.

BADASS RATING: ★★★★

ZHAO

Zhao Pingyang (598–623) sold her family's home when her father started a rebellion against the Sui Dynasty, using the money to build an army that led them to victory.

BADASS RATING: ★★★★

MORE ZANY Zs

ZORA

Zora Neale Hurston (1891–1960) was the extraordinary author and anthropologist who became the literary queen of the Harlem Renaissance.

BADASS RATING: ★★★★